KU-605-306

THE CHILDREN ACT REVIEW
A Scottish Experience

edited by Carolyn Martin

CLYDEBANK · DISTRICT LIBRARY

Children
IN SCOTLAND
CLANN AN ALBA
working for children and their families

EDINBURGH : HMSO

REF 344.0327

TITLE

9103

c 02 0140831

H.M.S.C
£22.5C
10.94

© Crown copyright 1994
First published 1994

Applications for reproduction should be made to HMSO

British Library Cataloguing in Publication Data
A catalogue record for this book is available from the British Library

ISBN 0 11 495244 2

About the Editor

Carolyn Martin, born in Edinburgh in 1950, is a graduate of Edinburgh University and obtained the Certificate of Education from Aberdeen College of Education in 1973. She taught infants in schools in Perth and Edinburgh before leaving teaching in 1977 to have a family, and returned to work in 1983 when she became the Scottish Development Officer for the National Playbus Association. A move to the Borders led to her appointment in 1990 as Children in Scotland's Borders Pre-Fives Development Officer, working on a collaborative multi-agency development project, completed in 1993. She is currently working for Borders College with a multi-agency consortium to develop a centre for SVQs in child care and education.

Acknowledgements

Children in Scotland and Carolyn Martin would like to offer sincere thanks to all those who contributed to this book. The project would not have been possible without their knowledge, expertise, and above all their willingness to make time in often hectic schedules to share their experiences.

CONTENTS

FOREWORD   xi

INTRODUCTION
Carolyn Martin   1

CHAPTER 1 GUIDING AND LEADING THE PROCESS   6
AN OVERVIEW   7
Cllr Elizabeth Maginnis, *Education Committee, COSLA*
STRATHCLYDE REGION   9
Cllr Tom Colyer, *Chair, Pre-Fives Education Sub-Committee*
BORDERS REGION   11
Cllr Nan Burnett, *Chair, Social Work Committee*
TAYSIDE REGION   12
Cllr Mervyn Rolfe, *Convener, Education Committee*
Cllr James Mudie, *Convener, Social Work Committee*
HIGHLANDS AND ISLANDS   14
WESTERN ISLES   14
Cllr Mary Bremner, *Social Work Committee*
Cllr Roderick MacDonald, *Education Committee*
SHETLAND ISLANDS   15
Cllr Leonard Groat, *Social Work Committee*
HIGHLAND REGION   16
Cllr Rev. Alexander Murray, *Social Work Committee*
ORKNEY ISLANDS COUNCIL   16
Cllr Alasdair Thom, *Social Work Committee*
Cllr Kathy Hutchison, *Education Committee*
GRAMPIAN REGION   17
Cllr Eric Hendrie, *Convener, Education Committee*
FIFE REGION   19
Cllr Charles Laing, *Convener, Social Work Committee*

CENTRAL REGION   19
Cllr Godfrey McIvor, *Convener, Education Committee*
LOTHIAN REGION   20
Cllr Brian Cavanagh, *Convener, Social Work Committee*

CHAPTER 2 WORKING THE PROCESS THROUGH
STRATHCLYDE REGION   23
Ronnie Hill, *Regional Development Officer, Pre-Fives Services*
Annette Holman, *Regional Adviser, Under-Fives*
TAYSIDE REGION   35
Ros Kirk, *Principal Officer, Children and Young People*
HIGHLAND REGION   51
Carole Taylor, *Regional Review Co-ordinator*
LOTHIAN REGION   59
Gary Pinnons, *Principal Officer (Children and Families)*
BORDERS REGION   64
Dr Sue Ross, *Assistant Director (Operations)*
Jimmy Hawthorn, *Principal Officer (Child Care)*

CHAPTER 3 BEING INVOLVED IN THE PROCESS   74
STRATHCLYDE REGION   74
Strathclyde Early Years Voluntary Sector Forum: Julie Collis
Strathclyde SPPA: Eileen McKenna
Scottish Childminding Association, Strathclyde: Marjorie Gregg
Lanarkshire Health Board: Helen Scott
Parks and Recreation Dept, Glasgow City Council: Ian Hooper
TAYSIDE REGION   78
Tayside SPPA: Catherine Murray
Tayside Health Board: M B Tannahill
HIGHLAND REGION   80
Scottish Childminding Association, Highland: Katie Adam
Highland SPPA: Ann Brady
BORDERS REGION   83
Borders Early Years Voluntary Sector Forum: Pat Newton
Borders SPPA: Pat Newton
Borders Health Board: Dr Adrian Margerison
LOTHIAN REGION   85
Lothian Community Child Health: Dr Patricia D Jackson
Sport and Recreation, East Lothian District Council: Alan Murray
Lothian SPPA: Barbara Stirling

CHAPTER 4 BEING CONSULTED ON THE PROCESS 89

Fife Play Partnership: Joan Pennycook
Grampian SPPA: Jacky Barrett
One Plus Strathclyde: John Findlay
Stepping Stones in Scotland: Anne Lancaster
Cothrom Centre South Uist: Mary Macinnes
Primrosehill Living Training Resource: Frances Littlejohn

CONCLUSION 101

Common Features of the Reviews Across Scotland
Information in the Reviews
Member Involvement and Policy Development
Policy Development and Inter-agency Work
Consultation
Effectiveness in Relating to Particular Groups
Quality and Training

BIBLIOGRAPHY 118

INDEX 121

FOREWORD

The early years of a child's life can be considered to be the most important because development and growth take place more rapidly than at any other stage in the lifecycle. The abilities of young children to learn, alongside their quest for new knowledge, will never be matched again in the course of their lives. The home and the child's wider environment are equally important to ensure that stability and stimulation are kept at an optimum.

Life chances for many children can be greatly enhanced through the experience of high quality daycare and education in these early years. It may take place in a variety of different settings such as family centres, nursery schools or classes, playgroups or private nurseries. It could be in the care of a trained and highly motivated childminder.

There is a weight of accumulating evidence which demonstrates that money invested in high quality pre-school services is money well spent. It has been shown to reduce the likelihood of offending behaviour, teenage pregnancies and to increase educational attainment. If it was more readily available at a price parents could afford then opportunities for women, particularly in lone parent families would be greatly increased. This would enable a greater contribution to be made to economic productivity and to the health and well-being of the whole family and the wider society while reducing dependency on the State.

The Children Act 1989 was welcomed in Scotland where, unlike England and Wales, the only aspects covered were the regulation and review of childminding, daycare and education services for children under eight. The rest of Scottish child care legislation has been dealt with separately and it was thought that bringing in this piece of new legislation, ahead of other changes, would give it higher public and political priority than might have otherwise been the case. This has been found to be true and the opportunity in Scotland has been grasped to increase knowledge and awareness of the issues which surround the provision of these services. Concern now must be expressed, however, about the general lack of integration which has become apparent in the approach to the changes in Scottish child care law and the effect of placing the provision, regulation and review of childminding, daycare and education services for young children outside these wider changes.

It must also be said that the impact of the Children Act has been limited by its primary concern with the local authority as regulator and reviewer, rather than provider of services. No additional central government funding was made available to assist with the new responsibilities resulting from the Act or to increase levels of services. The emphasis has therefore been, of necessity, on defining minimum standards and enforcing these to raise the quality of provision in all sectors. The focus on regulation has deflected attention away from other key issues around child care such as limited availability and access, low pay, conditions and status of carers and workers, the nature and extent of their training, etc. As a society we all carry responsibility for these matters as they reflect the relatively low priority we all give to children. Their care is seen as a private matter for parents rather than a social responsibility as it is in most other European countries. Quality has sometimes been forced into a back seat in the public eye when quantity appeared to be further threatened.

Local authorities throughout Scotland have used the Children Act Review of Childminding, Day Care and Education Services to take a much needed lead to begin to improve the situation for Scottish families. Despite the lack of additional resources from, and the lack of co-ordination by, central government, all Regional and Island Councils, without exception, recognised the importance of this issue and actively responded to the new legal duty to review childminding, daycare and education services within a very short space of time. It has been an extremely positive experience, overall. Social Work and Education Departments throughout Scotland have come together in a new and dynamic way. They have had to explore different ways of working together and with others, including parents. This has not always been an easy process and each authority has found its own solutions.

A variety of innovative means were employed to tackle the Review. This required local authorities to commit their own resources, necessitating diversions of funds from other high priority areas, to make sure it was done effectively. Many had to set up new mechanisms to improve collation and exchange of information about daycare. All authorities became involved in the publication of a major joint report which brought together information of a kind which had never been presented in this way before.

Some authorities became involved in publishing other information such as directories and parent information leaflets. Consultation meetings were set up with the public and representatives from other sectors. Some endeavours were more successful than others but time did not allow for a free-flow exchange of information between local authorities which would have been beneficial to all concerned. It should also be borne in mind that all the Review activity took place at the same time as Social Work Departments were required to implement new regulatory duties. It is, therefore, all the more commendable that the quality of the work produced, across the whole of Scotland, in the first Review was of such a high standard.

Many of these experiences will be shared through this book, making a valuable contribution to the development of future collaborative work. There is much to be learned about what works and what does not, not only for application in this field but in other areas where joint planning is essential.

The publication of a Review report is not an end in itself. It is only the beginning of an ongoing process of developing daycare and education services for young children. Further Review reports will be published every three years. This book will become a useful reference for future Reviews of services. It brings together the unique, as well as the common experiences of individual local authorities as they set about this work. We need to learn from each other to build a collective experience of building daycare and education policies and services for young children and their families. This book gives us a vehicle for doing this, making sure that valuable information of this kind is brought together to inform and improve the process for the future.

The book will also contribute to current debate and discussion around daycare and education for young children. This is essential to keep it as a public issue, high on the political agenda at a time of rapid change and unprecedented demands on resources. It is only through this that adequate investment can be made to increase the quality in, and levels of, all types of such services. It is in the interest of us all that this is done. Children are our investment in the future.

James M Mudie
Convenor of the Social Work Committee
Convention of Scottish Local Authorities

INTRODUCTION
Carolyn Martin

The benefits derived by children from access to high quality pre-school services have long been appreciated. Legislation early in the century empowered local authorities to establish nursery education, and since then research has highlighted the important contribution which high quality early childhood care and educational services can make to the social behaviour and educational and employment opportunities of children. [Schweinhart, L., Weikart, D. and Larner, M. (1986); Jowett, S. and Sylvia, R. (1986); Blackburne, L. (1992); Andersson, B.E. (1992)]. Recent (unfavourable) comparisons in levels of nursery education with other countries in the European Union have further stirred the debate. Scotland provides only just over a third of three- and four-year-olds with nursery education, predominantly in part-time places. By contrast, over 95% of French and Belgian three- and four-year-olds receive nursery education, generally on a full-time basis (CEC, 1990).

However the issue of early years services has also come to the fore through the growing debate over how to meet more effectively the needs of families caught up in what is often described as "family change" – substantial demographic, social and economic trends which are highlighting the need for enhanced family support. Smaller families can mean less help with childcare from adult relatives and siblings; one parent families now total 15.8% of families in Scotland and may have additional need of support. As the Government White Paper *Scotland's Children: Proposals for Child Care Policy and Law* published in August 1993 notes:

> Children now experience very diverse forms of family life as their parents
> co-habit, separate, marry and remarry. . . in this changing world, families
> will need support in ensuring a consistently high quality of care. *(Scottish
> Office 1993.)*

Change has also affected the environment within which many children are cared for. "Child unfriendly" housing conditions for some families, traffic and "stranger danger" for all families, have added to the need for services. The dangers posed by traffic and "stranger danger" have contributed to a substantial reduction in the number of activities children are able to undertake on their own. A PSI Survey comparing the independent mobility of English junior school children in 1971 and 1990 found a reduction by almost a half in the number of activities children were undertaking on their own (Hillman 1993).

However the factor within "family change" which has had the most significant implications for early years services has been a substantial rise in the number of women with young children entering the labour market or those who would wish to do so if appropriate services were available. In the United Kingdom as a whole the proportion of women with a child under ten in paid employment rose by 13% to 51% in the relatively short six-year period from 1985 to 1991. (CEC 1993). In Scotland the 1991 Census data shows that 43% of women with a child under five and 66% of women with a child aged 5–15 were economically active.

The convergence of these trends has brought an explosion in the demand for services. There has been no national survey of demand for services since 1974. The results of a more recent OPCS study are still unpublished. However, numerous local surveys and the evidence provided by the Reviews themselves show that the supply of services falls far short of both demand and need.

The reasons why families want services may vary. These include access to work or training, providing parents with time for themselves or contributing to the community in a variety of different ways, helping their children to learn and develop, to help overcome disabilities, and in some cases to provide access to a child's linguistic and cultural heritage. The reasons may vary but they add up to a very considerable and growing demand and need for services. All of the contributions to this book recognise, in varying degrees, the challenge which this presents to policy development at the level of both national and local government.

Growing demand for services has contributed to an increase in private sector provision, in particular childminding, nannies and private nurseries. Whilst these developments fall far short of filling the substantial gap between supply and demand they were responsible for some of the stresses and strains on existing legislation which led to its revision. For example the high costs of childcare led to "shared nanny" arrangements not recognised under existing legislation. Increasing use of private nurseries focused attention on their quality and a growing awareness of the need for out of school facilities drew attention to ineffective regulation in this area. These and other issues led to the revision of the 1948 Nurseries and Childminders Regulation Act. In England and Wales the revisions to this Act were contained within wider legislation in the form of the Children Act 1989, setting out the law on support services, daycare, family and care proceedings. Those provisions of this Act relating to the regulation of daycare apply to Scotland and came into force with the Children Act in October 1991. At the time that the legislation in England and Wales was enacted, Scottish legislation was expected to follow covering many of the other areas of the 1989 Act within the context of Scottish legal and welfare systems. In the event Scottish legislation has been substantially delayed. A number of the contributions within this book comment on the resulting vacuum surrounding what is described by Sue Ross and Jimmy Hawthorne in Chapter 2 "Borders Region", in this book as "the 'tartanisation' of a small part of the Children Act".

Those Sections of the 1989 Act relating to daycare and which apply in Scotland are Part X (Section 1–79) and Section 19 of Part III. Part X of the Act introduced provisions governing the registration and inspection of daycare services under which all daycare coming within the scope of the Act has to be registered with the Social Work Department and inspected on an annual basis. The initial registration of all provision was required to be completed within a year of the legislation coming into effect. Section 19 of the Act requires all local authorities to review the level, pattern and range of daycare provision within their areas on a three yearly basis. The first Review of Services for under eights was required to be available in draft form by October 1992.

The review provision within the Act was widely welcomed for providing an opportunity to explore needs and demand. Scottish Office guidance to local authorities specified that its central purpose "is to gather accurate information and to use it to increase interest in services for young children among the population as a whole, encourage debate about local services and how their development can produce benefits." (Scottish Office Guidance to Local Authorities, June 1991.) The strong emphasis on inter-agency collaboration as part of the review process was also seen as particularly valuable by many agencies.

The responsibility for carrying out the Review of Services for under eights is placed jointly within the Social Work and Education Departments, and it is made clear that the Review must be carried out "in consultation with health boards, voluntary organisations, employer interests, parents and other interested bodies and individuals".

In considering how the Review was implemented by Scotland's local authorities, it is important to recognise, as noted by Cllr Maginnis in her overview to Chapter 1, that local authorities were starting from very different points. It was not a level playing field. For example, the types of structures, particularly inter-agency structures, which were already in place and which could facilitate the Review, varied considerably from authority to authority. Some authorities were well used to taking an inter-agency view and had a history of multidisciplinary collaboration in the early years field which gave them a considerable head start. For other authorities, the process of working together on an inter-agency basis was very largely a new one. For these authorities, organising the Review required fundamental thinking on how to bring agencies together and how to carry through meaningful consultation.

In addition, there were differences across authorities in the amount of information they already had available to them – from registration and other departmental sources and through independent audits. For example, in the Borders a survey of services and demand for those services had been carried out shortly before the Review by Children in Scotland.

A number of factors contributed to the difficulties of local authorities in carrying out the reviews. These included:

- Uncertainty about future legislation in Scotland concerning child care law - to what extent would this provide a focus on children in need similar to the legislation in England and Wales?
- The stresses associated with the introduction of community care legislation.
- The imminent prospect of local government reorganisation.
- The absence of funding for carrying out the Review – very few authorities were able to create posts with the specific remit of co-ordinating the work and the process of consultation required by the Act was curtailed in many instances by the constraints imposed by the lack of funding and staffing resources to organise it effectively.

Taken together these factors meant that the climate was less than conducive to carrying out a major review of services for young children in the very short space of a year.

The timetable for the Review, coming as it did hard on the heels of the requirement to register all daycare within the regions, also caused difficulties for Social Work and Education Departments. The work was carried out by and large by staff who already had full workloads concerned with the wider aspects of their jobs. In these circumstances it was a not inconsiderable achievement that all local authorities in Scotland completed their first Review and, as required, published reports, in most cases very full reports, detailing the results. It is too soon to assess to what extent the process and findings of the Reviews have contributed to developing policies and improving services to any significant degree within local authorities. Many local authorities argue that resources are critical to this process and point to the need for a lead from central government.

In England and Wales, the changes relating to daycare services introduced in the Children Act 1989 have been the subject of systematic research – in major studies funded through the Department of Health and being carried out by the Thomas Coram Research Unit and the National Children's Bureau. This book is not the result of a similar study carried out in Scotland. It is, of necessity, a limited attempt to describe the process which was engaged in by local authorities throughout Scotland in carrying out their responsibility to review the level, pattern and range of daycare within their areas. It aims to give an experiential account from a number of different perspectives including local members, officers and other agencies in the independent sector. Contributors have considered the implications of the Review for quality and distribution of service provision, the implications for policy development and corporate planning and the likely effect on inter-agency working in the future.

The sequence followed in the book mirrors the process which the Review itself was required to follow, beginning with the setting of the terms of reference and the guidance which was required to be given by councillors, following through with the lead taken by Social Work and Education Departments and ending with the consultation required in the context of an inter-agency approach.

The book shares some of the lessons learned from this first Review with the aim of assisting future Reviews. In a wider context, by examining the inter-agency working required for the Review, the book provides insights into more general issues. These include communication, use of resources, monitoring and evaluating the effectiveness of service delivery, and policy development and strategic planning. An examination of these issues should assist in the planning process and lead to a more effective service for local communities.

It is hoped that the book will contribute to debate over how organisations from the statutory, voluntary and private sectors can best work together to maximise the benefits to the individuals and communities they serve and to improve the quality of provision in an increasingly important area of daily life.

Chapter 1

◆

GUIDING AND LEADING THE PROCESS

The Guidance on the Review of Services asks that the terms of reference for the Review be set by local authorities, involving members from Social Work and Education. In addition, members are asked to provide an oversight of the process itself; but is the requirement to review services for young children likely to lead to changes in levels of political awareness, policy development or corporate planning and how do local politicians themselves view their role in the Review?

In examining the review process it is important to consider these questions from a political perspective. Any increase in provision for young children, or better targeting and improvements in the quality of existing care, is dependent on a political understanding of the purpose of the Review and a commitment to and acceptance of the importance of services for young children. It requires a willingness to respond to the findings of the Review, at both a national and a local level, by a re-examination of policies and priorities where necessary and an allocation of appropriate resources where they are needed.

All conveners of Social Work and Education Committees throughout Scotland were invited to consider these questions. Responses indicated that the process of carrying out the Review had been a very diverse one for politicians and the degree of involvement and knowledge as to the Review process varied considerably from authority to authority.

In general it would appear that the smaller authorities, including those which are island based or with predominantly rural populations, carried out the Review with only very limited member involvement, usually confined to a consideration of draft documents, once these were made available by officers. However, even in these small authorities, where difficulties associated with member involvement revolve around such issues as geographical distance, expense, lack of time and other priorities, there is a recognition that the first Review was a learning process. Member involvement will require to be more clearly defined against agreed terms of reference in time for future Reviews so that there can be a clarity of role which many authorities felt was missing first time round.

Notwithstanding these teething problems, all authorities report the Review as being a positive experience which has not only provided valuable information which will be of use in determining future policy and practice in the under eights field, but also has forged new and important relationships across committees. These relationships will facilitate future planning towards a cohesive and comprehensive early years service in Scotland.

AN OVERVIEW
Cllr Elizabeth Maginnis, Education Committee, COSLA[1]

The opportunity to review services for the under eights was generally welcomed across Scotland. It was recognised that the Review would allow the evaluation and assessment of current provision in the public, voluntary and private sectors.

It was intended that the Review would be carried out using a multidisiplinary approach involving providers, policy makers, practitioners and users. Positive developments would be recognised and gaps in current provision could be identified. The guidelines produced by The Scottish Office did not give any clear indications of how this Review should be approached by local authorities. There was no increase in funding to cover the cost of the Review, resulting in local authorities having to divert resources to pay for it.

All local authorities in Scotland were starting the Review from a different position. Some had already established multidisciplinary teams, with officers from both Social Work and Education Departments working together on the provision of services, particularly for the under fives (with the introduction of the Act some extended their remit to include services for the under eights), others had to develop such teams. The position was reflected too in staffing terms with some regions creating development officer posts to oversee the Review while others seconded officers from Social Work and/or Education Departments.

In elected member terms there were differences in their approach to the Review. Administrations have different structures for identifying and developing policies for the under eights. Prior to the Review, advisory groups on pre-five services were used in the Borders and Central Regions, and a joint sub committee on services for the under fives was in operation in Strathclyde Region. Tayside and Dumfries & Galloway set up joint forums specifically for the Review. Voluntary organisations, representatives from the private sector and individual users were also to be included in the Review.

[1] I am deeply indebted to Councillor Margaret McCulloch, Chair of Lothian Regional Council's Joint Under Fives Committee, who conducted the review and whose experience provided much of the text for this contribution.

The variation between authorities is reflected in the differences both in the membership of the teams set up to work on the Review and in the process of reporting the outcome to a formal committee. Throughout the country membership of the teams included officers from both Social Work and Education Departments but varied on inclusion of elected members, voluntary organisations, private sector and health board representatives and only one team (Tayside) included a parent.

The intention of the Review was to conduct a full scale audit of services provided by local authorities, voluntary organisations and the private sector. However, the time scale laid down by The Scottish Office was insufficient to carry this out effectively. Changes to the registration and inspection legislation were being implemented by local authorities at the same time as the Review was being conducted. This meant that registration and inspection units were not all fully operational by the time of the Review. The next Review, when it is anticipated that better information will be available from the registration and inspection units, will be of improved quality as a result. It was possible this time round to obtain information about existing groups and childminders registered under previous legislation but this did not apply to groups such as mothers and toddlers, after school clubs, play schemes and creches.

The guidelines for the Review indicated that, in order to include the services available in the voluntary sector, identify gaps in service provision and reflect the needs of users of the services, wide ranging consultation with these groups, as well as individuals, was an integral part of the review process. The guidelines were, however, unspecific about how this consultation was to be achieved. Carrying out this part of the Review highlighted the lack of appropriate channels through which views can be expressed. Various methods were used by different authorities, reflecting in some part the differences in geographic location.

There was general dissatisfaction with this part of the Review. Too many people and groups were excluded, due to time factors and the absence of information regarding their whereabouts. In particular there was a lack of information about minority ethnic groups, special needs groups and parents who have little or no access to childcare and who were not represented by any organisation. In most regions it will be necessary to establish a comprehensive information base taking into account the range of special interest groups. This information has to be accessible to policy makers, providers, planners and users.

What is not certain is how the results of these Reviews will be used. A number of issues have been highlighted which will have to be addressed by organisations and by politicians. Thought has to be given as to how future consultation is arranged, taking into account differences in geographic area, population mixes and how service users are to be heard. While the Review did strengthen the links between the various participants, existing structures were not able to meet the requirements of the review process. This will have to be addressed before undertaking future Reviews.

All of the Reviews have highlighted gaps in service provision and while costs involved to both service providers and to users have not been included in the Review there is general agreement that it will not be possible to increase services to close these gaps unless there is a commitment from The Scottish Office to increase funding to local authorities. The funding must be specifically designated for services for the under eights.

Involvement in the process of the reviews by voluntary organisations and individuals has heightened expectations of an improvement in the quality, range and availability of services. Gaps in provision do exist all over Scotland in all sectors of under eight provision and a failure to act on the information gained by this review process will be clearly evident when the process is repeated again in three years time.

It is clear that if the Secretary of State intends this Review to be more than simply a national audit, he must use the information gathered to inform his national policy statements. Equally, it is clear that an unambiguous commitment to more resources is essential if services to the under eights are to be coherently developed. Perhaps the key to his whole approach must be, though, a fundamental acknowledgement that each sector – private, voluntary and public agencies – has important and unique contributions to make to the necessarily wide and varied choices available for parents. No single sector can provide for all the responsibilities and challenges implicit in services for the under eights – the Secretary of State's policy statement must reflect and value each sector's contribution.

STRATHCLYDE REGION
Cllr Tom Colyer, Chair, (Pre-Fives) Education Subcommittee

The need to conduct a comprehensive review of education, childminding and daycare services for children under eight presented local authorities with a number of considerable challenges. Information on population levels, patterns of need and on levels of provision available in defined areas had to be gathered and assembled. An audit of provision which would inform the planning of future service development and provide parents and other interested individuals and organisations with detailed, comprehensive information was to be produced. Consultation on policy, the nature of provision needed and the possible means of expanding services, was to be undertaken with parents, providers and other authorities and organisations involved in the care and education of young children, and in the support of families.

The timing of the first Review, falling within a year of the implementation of Part X of the Children Act in Scotland, meant that this work had to be undertaken by local authorities which were also busy at that time developing and putting into practice new procedures for registration and inspection of daycare. Limited additional financial assistance was given to local authorities by central government for the conduct of the Review, and for implementation of registration and inspection. Despite this, Strathclyde Regional Council employed a further 12.5 pre-school community organisers, together with clerical assistants, at a cost of £250,000, to meet the increased workload arising from registration duties. Key staff in Strathclyde were diverted from other responsibilities to gather and assemble the information for the Review reports and to conduct an extensive programme of consultation, at regionwide and local levels. As a result, certain other areas of work were disrupted and delayed. It is to the credit of the staff involved in the Review under these circumstances and against the very tight time scales imposed by central government, that the work was undertaken in an efficient, effective manner.

Collaboration between departments within Strathclyde Regional Council, the voluntary sector, and other providers of services for children under eight was, I believe, a strong feature of the strategy adopted for the conduct of the Review within this regional council's area. The structures for such collaboration were firmly laid in Strathclyde Region when social work and education provision for under fives and their families were brought together under the management of the Director of Education.

The Education (Pre-Five) Sub Committee had been formed in Strathclyde to oversee this area of work. This Committee, which consists of councillors from the Education and Social Work Committees of the council, set the terms of reference for the Review and monitored its progress. The voluntary sector is also represented on the Committee. Through this involvement, and by other means, the voluntary sector took an active part in the Review of Services in Strathclyde. As Chair of this Committee I have, together with my fellow councillors, been keen to promote collaboration, partnership and consultation on the policies relating to the provision of services and on the means of enhancing the range, quantity and quality of these services.

This commitment was underlined by Strathclyde Regional Council when, earlier this year, it approved the final report on the Review of Services for children under eight. This council's commitment to working in partnership with others to develop further the number and range of services made available is also restated in this document.

In the period since the Review was published, this Regional Council has approved the establishment of a further 316 full time equivalent nursery places for children aged 0–5 years at a cost of some £500,000 per year. This is a very considerable achievement for this authority, particularly at this time of severe economic restraint. However, the increase appears modest indeed when set against the known shortfall in the total level of the provision which is required. It is estimated, for example, that if this present rate of increase in the number of nursery places is maintained, there will be a place for all children whose parents require it in 75 years time!

It seems quite clear to me, as I am sure it must to others, that this is too long to wait. The opportunities presented by this Review to raise the profile of services for young children and to advocate for the release of adequate central government resources to fund it must be grasped. The Review documents must not be allowed to remain on the shelf to gather dust. Information on the range and level of need for services which the report contains should be used to advocate for planned and coordinated childcare provision to be made available for all who require it.

BORDERS REGION
Cllr Nan Burnett, Chair, Social Work Committee

Early in the 1980s Borders Regional Council declared its commitment to developing services for the under fives. In 1987 a joint report to the Social Work and Education Committees resulted in agreement to a set of shared priorities and objectives and the setting up of a multi-agency Working Party for Under Fives (WORPUF).

As part of the Council's commitment to early years work, it supported the Children in Scotland Early Years Development Project which focused on the needs of under eights in a multidisciplinary, collaborative way. The *Family Matters* report, published in 1991 by Children in Scotland as part of that project, gave us a detailed analysis of the wishes of many families with young children in the Borders. This report provided valuable source material for the Review of Services for under eights. In addition, elected members attending the seminar which launched the report asked many questions which will help the formulation of policy, the need for which was underlined in the Review, approved by Social Work and Education Committees in November 1992.

Many of our hopes have not been realised. The Children in Scotland Early Years Development Project ended in June 1993 and, so far, we have not been able to fund another post. The commitment remains, however, to the policy objectives stated in the Review document.

The Review process has strengthened an already meaningful partnership between departments and committees of the Council, especially Social Work and Education. Relationships have improved, too, between public and private provision, the voluntary and statutory sectors and between officers and elected members.

A number of serious difficulties and indeed challenges remain, not least of which is the reorganisation of local government and the continuing constraints on finance. There are, however, some opportunities, and the requirement to review services three years on gives a focus to assess progress. It will be important to build on the growing good relationships and to grasp the opportunities afforded by new training initiatives for childcare workers. But probably most importantly of all, we need to capitalise on the growing power of families to articulate their need for facilities in this rural area and use it to place their needs higher up the political agenda. There is still much to be done but there is a commitment to this work.

TAYSIDE REGION
Cllr Mervyn Rolfe, Convener, *Education Committee*
Cllr James Mudie, Convener, *Social Work Committee*

Councillors Rolfe and Mudie both responded to the invitation to contribute to the book in keeping with the Tayside response to the Review, which was to use it as a way of tying the two strands of Social Work and Education more closely together. Here they consider why the authority set up a Joint Regional Under Eights Co-ordinating Group and what its particular benefits were; how far local members were involved in the Review process; what they felt the benefits in policy development terms were likely to be; and how inter-agency working and the Review as a whole may affect service developments for early years in the future.

Tayside Regional Council has been particularly innovative in its approach to the implementation of the Children Act 1989. It was recognised by the members that an entirely new mechanism required to be set up – a Joint Regional Under Eights Co-ordinating Group with membership including the Conveners and Vice-Conveners of both Committees. This group has been responsible for overseeing the implementation of the Children Act with particular reference to the requirement to review and report on the level, pattern and range of daycare and related services for young children.

It does not have the authority of a Committee, and some reports have therefore had to go to the full Committees. However, the existence of this group does enable members to give more time and priority to early years issues.

To ensure that the information under consideration by members represented the views of parents and providers from other sectors, a Working Group representing those interests was set up at the same time. Demands on members' time did not allow the setting up of a joint member/officer group and this was seen as an alternative. Now that local consultation fora are being established which also represent similar interests to those on the Working Group, its role needs to be reviewed and this is likely to begin in the near future.

In addition to the setting up of new political and inter-departmental officer structures, it was seen as essential to make a number of new appointments to cover regulation and review duties. The resource implications resulting from the Children Act were far greater for the Social Work Department than Education because of responsibilities for regulation - £200,000 compared to £50,000. As there was no money available from either central government or from within existing departmental funds, a political case had to be made within the Regional Council to secure this money from other general funds. This was successfully achieved and the Social Work Department appointed officers to undertake new regulatory duties and a Development Officer to work alongside a newly created mirror post in the Education Department on the Review. The Education Department also appointed a Training Co-ordinator to work inter-departmentally and across sectors, in recognition of the importance of the training agenda to the issue.

Members must balance the needs of the community across a spectrum of needs and must make the final decisions about the allocation of scarce resources. Had effective collaborative structures not been established, along with sound planning information, elected representatives would be unable to make a convincing case for the allocation of resources in this area.

Political support was essential to secure the funds necessary for successful implementation. Similarly, the joint political involvement set the scene and expectations for further collaboration at officer level.

It is necessary to be aware of potential difficulties such as raised parental expectations of additional services in a particular area. There may be clashes of interests between providers and those regulating services who may be trying to raise standards. In responding to these it is important that members have access to sound information about existing provision and base the planning of all types of development in which daycare has a bearing on well informed planning information.

Daycare serves a number of purposes. Different departments tend to emphasise one aspect more than another. A collaborative approach and increased understanding helps bring together these perspectives which are not as divergent as they sometimes might appear.

The involvement of members is likely to mean a fuller awareness when difficult decisions about resource allocations require to be made. It also provides as direct a link as possible to the democratic process. The infrastructure of co-ordinating group, working group and development officers should also be able to inform the development of future policies. The nature of the joint venture, involving constant consultation with and involvement of members and officers from more than one department, will facilitate the process of corporate planning by providing a basis for common understanding.

It was the decision of members to restrict involvement to the Regional Co-ordinating Group because of the pressure of other demands. The disadvantage of this is that it is not possible to be as involved in the detail of policy recommendations as one might have liked. The onus is on the officers to keep members informed. They may be selective about this. There have not been any difficulties to date.

Currently the involvement of members is confined to the co-ordinating group and it may be worth considering the benefits of member involvement at working group level.

The Review was not a one-off exercise and therefore there is a continuing need for political and departmental co-ordination. It will change and develop over time. The Review has the potential to raise public expectations which can be difficult given the unprecedented demands on public funding and the forthcoming plans for local government reorganisation. These pressures are not likely to make the daycare situation better unless it becomes a major issue on the political agenda, in response to public opinion or economic demands. It becomes increasingly difficult to secure resources for longer term gain when the national political situation is uncertain.

The next Review is due in 1995. This could mean provision of daycare services will be high on the political agenda at the time of local government elections and local government reorganisation. It will certainly ensure that this provision remains firmly on the political agenda.

HIGHLANDS AND ISLANDS

In addition to more general difficulties experienced by all authorities, particularly related to changing legislation in other fields, political involvement within Regional and Islands Councils in the Highlands and Islands area appears to have been characterised by particular difficulties associated with geography and consequent lengthy travel distances to meetings. This, in addition to prohibitive costs, has tended to limit the scope of the direct involvement of members.

However, there is also the view expressed by one Council, that being a single tier authority actually facilitates decision-making and made the process less complicated.

Western Isles
Cllr Mary Bremner, *Social Work Committee*
Cllr Roderick MacDonald, *Education Committee*

Member involvement in the review process in the Western Isles was limited to the final document, which was drafted by a working group of officers from the appropriate departments of the Council, being submitted to the Social Work and

Education Committees for approval. Given that the initial document was required to be prepared within a very short timescale, and the fact that it took the form of a directory of services throughout the Western Isles, it was considered that member involvement, at that stage, was unnecessary.

The 1995 document will require us to provide more detailed information in terms of policies and provision of services within the various departments of the Council. Because of this, it will be necessary for member involvement at an earlier stage, and we would envisage a working party of appropriate members and officers being established to prepare the draft document before it is submitted to the Social Work Committee and the Education Committee for approval.

In addition to the limitations on member involvement caused by the very short timescale involved, another consideration, in relation to the Western Isles, is the geographical location of council members, which makes it extremely difficult, and very expensive, for members to be involved in working party meetings. In overcoming these problems, we normally try and schedule such meetings to coincide with the normal Council Committee and Sub-Committee meetings, in order to reduce expenditure and ease the burden on members in terms of time commitments and absences away from home.

The requirement to review services for under eights every three years will inevitably lead to a much higher profile for services for the under eights. The Review will require the Council to consider the provision of services required and assess the resource implications which have to be allocated in order to implement an adequate level of service within the Western Isles.

Shetland Islands

Cllr Leonard Groat, Social Work Committee

In Shetland the major benefit of the Review seems to have been the improvement in the knowledge and understanding it brought about amongst councillors.

The purpose of the Review was to provide information about the existence of services and raise issues concerning provision and, in Shetland, members noted this. Their involvement was limited to debates within the political process. However, it is undoubtedly the case that the Review has raised the profile of services for the under eights and members are much clearer about the existence of services and developments in this area as a result.

The ramifications of reviewing every three years will be to raise public awareness and heighten further the profile which will impinge on the political process. There will inevitably be a greater demand to improve services by the public.

Highland Region

Cllr Rev. Alexander Murray, Social Work Committee

Member involvement in Highland Region was simply in the way of providing an overview of the process. At its meeting of 29 April, 1992, the Social Work Committee extended the remit of the Special Sub-Committee for Pre-school Provision to include under eights and renamed it the Joint Sub-Committee for Provision for the Under Eights. Members are drawn from both Education and Social Work Committees. The Committee was to discuss the Review and also the White Paper, once it was published. The Committee delegated responsibility for carrying out the Review to officers and its role has been to consider the draft and pass it on to the full Committee.

Highland is a non-party political Council where councillors are elected in the main as independents and in that respect is not affected in the political realm to the extent that other councils are. One can envisage a lack of continuity in the members' overseeing of the issues in respect of plans for reorganisation; although, again, if the present plan holds, that may not be so acute in Highland.

Orkney Islands Council

Cllr Alasdair Thom, Social Work Committee
Cllr Kathy Hutchison, Education Committee

Member involvement in the process of Review of Day Care and Education Services for Under Eights has been restricted for a number of reasons, primarily the relatively low priority the council members have been able to afford this matter in the face of so much changing legislation during the current term.

Individual members are aware of the need for under eight provision within their constituencies and certainly the development of nursery school provision is proceeding. Similarly, childminding facilities are recognised as providing an important resource within neighbourhoods and communities.

The Orkney Islands Council as a single tier local authority has certain advantages in that it has an easier decision-making process. However, because of its size, resources are more critical, particularly between service priorities both within and across Departments. One of the consequences of this situation has been the need to work more closely with outside agencies and organisations who also have to deal with critical resource issues, to establish and provide facilities which the individual agency could not fund on its own.

The Council currently has no corporate policy on the provision of services for under eights. The Review has highlighted the need for greater cooperation between the Education Department and the Social Work Department specifically in the area of policy development and service planning. This has been acknowledged and the Council has set up a Sub-Committee to consider matters affecting both Committees and to develop policies of mutual interest. The Sub-

Committee has yet to meet but even at this stage there is already recognition of a potential inconsistency in the standards and regulations applied by the Education Act and the Children Act. While the introduction of the Sub-Committee will go some way to dealing with aspects of mutual interest, both Departments still have to be considered separately by the two Committees.

The political ramifications of the requirement to review services for under eights every three years are principally the need for a more formal approach to these services, the need to consider the matter of supply and demand and the consequences these might have for the allocation of resources and finally the development of purchaser/provider arrangements.

GRAMPIAN REGION
Cllr Eric Hendrie, *Convener, Education Committee*

In planning for the Review of Day Care Services for Children Under Eight senior officials from the Education and Social Work Departments met to establish the parameters of the Review and to agree upon an appropriate means of conducting it. It was agreed that the Development Officer for Day Care Services for the Under Eights from the Social Work Department, with the assistance of the Pre-school Services Development Officer from the Education Department would:

1. Form a Consultative Committee consisting of representatives from Education, Health, Social Work, Scottish Childminding Association, Scottish Pre-school Play Association and the private sector.
2. This Committee to meet and identify issues of central importance to each group.
3. To substantiate these issues with data and narrative explaining why they were important and/or problematic and how they might best be addressed in the future.
4. To identify and note secondary issues to which consideration ought to be given in the future.
5. Within 2, 3 and 4 to consult with parents, disability and special needs groups and ethnic minority communities and thereby to identify issues relevant to these groups and to ensure they receive proper priority.
6. To issue a report which would be a position statement and suggest an agenda for future discussions.

A number of issues were discussed and it became apparent that most of the representatives on the Review Consultative Committee shared the same concerns. At the same time the Development Officer contacted a large number of voluntary organisations. A questionnaire for parents was distributed. The process of consultation was carried out during the months of June to August. This period coincided with the long summer holiday break. It was acknowledged that this timing was unfortunate, albeit unavoidable.

The issue of information and consultation was particularly highlighted. The private and voluntary sectors felt they had been overlooked by the Council in setting up its guidelines to Part X of the Act and, to some extent this reflected the timescale within which the Council had to operate. However, the Review process proved to be extremely beneficial and a number of important contacts were made as a result. It was recognised that the onus would be on the Council to maintain and develop these contacts to ensure that the community be actively involved in the future.

It was also clear that the Act had significant implications for both the Education and Social Work Departments and there needed to be joint understanding of this. Both Departments functioned under different governing legislation and brought a different professional perspective to pre-eights provision. It was agreed that greater clarity was needed in understanding the roles and responsibilities of each Department in respect of the new legislation.

The Council established a Joint Consultative Group, accountable to the Social Work and Education Committees of the Council and comprising of regional councillors, senior officers of the Social Work and Education Departments and appropriate outside bodies.

In considering the area of daycare services for children under eight a number of Action Areas have been identified by the Joint Consultative Group which reflect the outcomes of the Review:

1. Establish liaison arrangements between Education and Social Work Departments.
2. Establish communication structures.
3. Investigate and report upon access to provision.
4. Investigate and report upon the balance of funding for under eight provision.
5. Investigate and report upon training.
6. Prepare guidelines in relation to definitions of quality.
7. Investigate and report upon children with special needs.
8. Investigate and report upon ethnic minorities.
9. Investigate and report upon after school care.
10. Investigate and report upon the needs of parents.

In progressing the above Action Areas it is clear that the scale of the task will involve exploration and consideration of those areas over a short-, mid- and longer-term period. Within the short-term, action has already been taken and work initiated by an inter-departmental officer group in response to areas 1. – 5.

One of the stated aims of the Joint Consultative Group is to "develop a common philosophy with respect to pre-eight provision which will utilise the skills and expertise of each Department and enable the Departments to work in a complementary way when promoting high quality childcare within the

Region". At the same time it has been a clear intention of the Review to ensure that the knowledge and experience of the community as a whole be utilised in deciding how best to provide for the children of Grampian.

It is felt that the experience of the Review and its outcomes has been to set in place a process of on-going consultation, development and review which will hopefully have a positive effect on this important area of childcare provision.

FIFE REGION
Cllr Charles Laing, Convener, Social Work Committee

In September 1991 the Social Work Committee was made aware of the requirement under Section 19 of the Children Act 1989 to review daycare services for children under eight. A consultative group composed of representatives from the Social Work Department, Education Department and Fife Health Board was set up to complete the report. It was not thought necessary to involve members directly at this stage as much of the work of the group would involve the collation of information. The draft report was presented separately to the Social Work Committee on 7 August and the Education Committee on 30 August 1992. After a period of consultation the final report was again presented to both committees before being published. It will be necessary to review the mechanisms for involving members in the process of preparing subsequent reports.

Fife's Section 19 Review Report refers directly to other policy and planning documents such as *A Plan for Fife, The Charter for Under Fives, Towards 2000* and the *Community Care Plan.* In doing this it locates daycare services for young children within the context of Fife Regional Council's overall policies and priorities. This will hopefully assist in the process of policy development and corporate planning. 2,157 parents of young children responded to the draft and outlined the services they required. We were very pleased with this level of response and these views will be crucial when developing policies and planning services.

The requirement to undertake these reviews has focused people's attention on daycare services for young children. The parents who have made their requirements known will be expecting services to be developed. This will not be easy to achieve in an environment of increasing financial constraint. There will also be organisational ramifications in the move towards single tier local authority status in 1996.

CENTRAL REGION
Cllr Godfrey McIvor, Convener, Education Committee

In April 1992 Central Regional Council set up a temporary Review team of one full time Review Officer from Social Work and one Review Officer (half-time) from Education. The work of the team was overseen by a steering group consisting of the Regional Convener, the Social Work Convener and Education Convener, together with representatives of departmental management. The first meeting with elected members took place on 10 September 1992; these meetings continued until December 1992.

The purpose was to ensure political direction and co-ordination of the exercises. Members were closely involved in considering and agreeing drafts of the Review document. The process ran in parallel with a major review of Pre-Fives policy in Central Region carried out by a member-officer group (Pre-Fives Policy Group).

Political awareness of the poor level of co-ordination of under eights services was heightened by involvement. In addition it provided the basis for better collaborative working and more co-ordinated policy development in the future. This is further helped in Central Region by the work of the Pre-Fives Policy Group.

One of the main limitations on the exercise was that a large amount of elected member time was already being devoted to the Pre-Fives Policy Group process. Another limitation was that much of the Children Act Review process was about basic information gathering; the scope for direct member involvement in this aspect is fairly limited.

In consideration of the ramifications of the triennial requirement to review much will depend on the future shape of service for under eights in Central Region. There is clearly a need for better political – and management – co-ordination of services. Central Regional Council is currently addressing this need during consideration of its consultation report on Pre-Fives Policy.

LOTHIAN REGION
Cllr Brian Cavanagh, Convener, Social Work Committee

The introduction of the Children Act 1989 put elected members in a bit of a quandary. The Act provided many councillors with a piece of legislation to put into practice many of their aspirations for young children. It enabled a debate to take place and a chance to review and reassess the activities of a range of services for young children.

The opportunity to review services for the under eights was welcomed throughout Scotland, not least in that it enabled an equal valuation of public, private and voluntary sector providers. In theory it presented an ideal opportunity to publicise examples of best practice worthy of export and identify gaps in service provision. The reality is that most local authorities started the Review from widely differing bases, both in the reporting and managing of under eight services.

For some authorities the responsibility lay with one department and committee, for example, Education. For others, such as Lothian, where both Social Work and Education have large budgets and a political commitment to identifying services, it necessitated a multidisciplinary officer team reporting to a Review or advisory committee.

Not only did the involvement and role of the officers and the departments vary from authority to authority, there was also the expectation that other providers, not least in the private and voluntary sectors, should participate in any advisory groups as well as representatives of users of services.

The role of members throughout Scotland has been extremely variable. Under fives services policy development is determined by how local authorities organise their committee structures. For example, Lothian's Joint Under Five Committee has been in operation since 1985 and includes membership from the Social Work, Education, and Women's Committee and the Health Board. In Strathclyde an Education Committee Sub-Committee is the main decision body. Tayside and Dumfries & Galloway have only recently set up joint fora for the Review.

It is true to say that the drive behind much of the day to day work in the Review process was not led by senior members of the ruling administration. Whilst provision in many authorities for under fives and under eights has a high political salience, senior members tend to see the "nuts and bolts" as left to backbench councillors. In some "traditional" authorities it is patronisingly referred to as a "women's issue". Membership of Review groups has often been made up of backbenchers acting under the aegis of their Chair, or people who were encouraged to participate and "make it their own issue".

The benefits from the participation of elected members in the process are considerable. It brings to the fore debates about quality – not just to be couched in terms of standards, but, more importantly, locating good quality services for the under eights at the centre of Councils' corporate strategies such as Anti-Poverty Programmes, Positive Discrimination Programmes and Return to Work Programmes.

In addition, it gives members a clear understanding of the issues around implementation. Too often in Scotland, councillors can have a traditional role of "councillors proposing, officers disclosing," assuming that because a decision has been made it will operate sweetly. The involvement in the Review has given councillors an insight into the gap between policy and implementation.

There are, however, some problems about member involvement. Involvement can be very sketchy and intermittent. As Review groups are without budgetary powers and advisory, they are not regarded as influential by senior politicians. They often do not have the appropriate Chair on the committee. The groups are often served by middle grade staff who do not have political clout. It is often the case that their work has to go through a sieve of senior officials before it meets the elected members.

The process may result in members becoming unhappy about the nature of reviews if the primary objective of improving the quality of service results in a number of long established groups, for example after school clubs, being unable to meet increasingly strict criteria and, as a result, provision is unable to be sustained.

If the debate becomes so focused and detailed that it becomes an officers' "talking shop", members will either be sucked into inappropriate activities or lose interest. Indeed it can result, and has resulted, in members losing sight of their role and encroaching on the role of officers.

In conclusion, the ramifications for a Review every three years are enormous. Councillors could be faced with having to de-register or close down an increasing number of services which don't meet the criteria on standards. The alternative would be for councillors to become prisoners of existing resources rather than trying to maintain high-quality provision. As a result the debate about high standards and a possible net reduction in service at a time when demand for under eights services is at an all time high, could be a political time bomb.

As the restrictions on local authority budgets increase, there will be a dramatic growth in the private sector to take up the slack in under eights provision, particularly at the nursery and childminding end. As these private sector providers become more powerful they might try to see a reduction in standards as a means of creating more provision. The battle for quality versus quantity represents a false dichotomy but may become increasingly a real one in the years to come. If local government is reorganised, the ability of new smaller authorities to have the necessary expertise to monitor, assess, check and review the provision of key services for the under eights must surely be questioned. The quality of services and all the gains achieved since the Children Act came into force could be put in jeopardy.

Chapter 2

◆

WORKING THE PROCESS THROUGH

STRATHCLYDE REGION
Ronnie Hill, *Regional Development Officer Pre-Fives Services*
Annette Holman, *Regional Adviser, Under Fives*

Background Information on Strathclyde

Services for children under eight are provided in a region of great diversity including remote rural areas and densely populated urban localities. Just over 10% of a population of 2 million is under eight – some 236,673, and 6% is under five. The distribution of population is not spread evenly across the six administrative divisions of the education department (see Fig. 2.1) nor is the spread of provision even, in either quantity or type. For example Glasgow has half the total number of creches in the region but only 13.7% of the playgroups.

Figure no. 2.1 Population of divisions as percentage of total regional population.

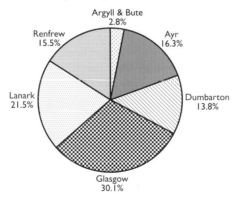

Fig. 2.2 (page 24) gives regional details of the numbers of services for children 0–5 years which are registerable under the Act and Fig. 2.3 gives similar data for children 5–8 years.

Figure no. 2.2 Number of Services in the independent sector across the region.

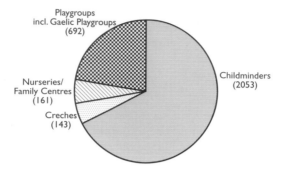

Figure no. 2.3.

	Playschemes	Out of School Scheme
Argyll and Bute	0	0
Ayr	62	6
Dunbarton	23	21
Glasgow	146	29
Lanark	97	7
Renfrew	21	11
	349	74

In 1986, Strathclyde Regional Council implemented its decision to bring all its pre-five services and the responsibility for the registration of childminders and playgroups under the direction of the Education Department. It also set up the Pre-Five Committee as a sub-committee of the Education Committee, with half its members drawn from that committee and half from the Social Work Committee. The voluntary sector was given representation, now arranged through the Strathclyde Early Years Voluntary Sector Forum, the establishment of which was agreed by the Pre-Five Sub-Committee in its first year. The Committee is attended by officers of the council drawn from the Education, Social Work, Chief Executive, Legal, Personnel Services and Architect's Departments. A Health Board representative is also a member. Thus prior to the Children Act, a formal structure for discussion of policy issues was in existence.

In April 1986, the Director of Education was empowered to carry out the functions of the council under the Nursery and Childminders Regulation Act 1948. The day to day work of registration was the responsibility of 35 pre-school community organisers (PSCOs) who had been based in the Social Work Department. Each division also had a newly appointed Pre-Five Development Officer. In the case of Argyll and Bute and Dumbarton Divisions, this was a shared post. PSCOs and Development Officers are managed by the Education Officer with responsibility for pre-fives services. Since 1986, there have been two increases in the staffing complement of PSCOs taking them to a total of 52. There has also been an increase in administrative support.

In August 1986, the Pre-Five Committee agreed to the establishment of a working party on childminding. The working party, with membership drawn from Education, Social Work, Legal Services and the voluntary sector recommended new registration procedures and an improvement in support for childminders. In August 1987, the new procedures were agreed, as was an increase in staffing in January 1988. A working party on creche registration was also set up and its work became incorporated into the broader review of registration which was undertaken in the light of the impending Children Act. This early work on registration proved very valuable because it anticipated some of the changes suggested in the draft and final guidelines on the Children Act and brought people together so that working relationships were forged before implementation of the Act and the planning of the triennial Review. Pre-five staff at headquarters also became involved in a working party on after-school care which again made links between personnel of different departments/agencies which proved helpful when the draft guidance on the Act was issued.

In March 1991, a working group on the Act was set up which also divided into sub groups to deal with the following themes:

- Procedures for registration, inspection, refusals, and appeals
- Staffing and resources
- Liaison between Education and Social Work
- Publicity about the Act for a number of audiences, parents, professionals, providers
- Training
- The triennial Review

The sub-group on the Review comprised initially members of the Education and Social Work Departments and the voluntary sector. In April 1991, they met and drew up an agenda for further discussions and work. The early establishment of the sub-group was important because it set a framework for the future which could be kept in mind while the more immediate issues of registration, staffing etc were addressed. The eventual production of a Review was an element in the discussions of many of the other sub-groups.

Another development within the region which was of value when the Review was carried out was the establishment of admissions panels containing representatives of local nurseries, social work staff, health visitors, psychological services and voluntary organisations to ensure that the application of the admissions policy to pre-five establishments is appropriate to the local area. Strathclyde also has approximately 100 Link-Up groups – informal locally based groups of parents, carers and those who work with children under six and their families. They meet regularly and work together to improve local services for children and their families to promote co-operation between existing services and to share information. They are supported by the Strathclyde Link Up Development and Training Project. These initiatives mean that at a local level there have been opportunities for people to come together and consider service provision and need.

Other liaison arrangements were well established in advance of the Act. The role of the pre-five committee has already been discussed. In addition, the chair, vice chair and delegated councillors hold quarterly meetings with the Strathclyde Early Years Voluntary Sector Forum. A separate set of meetings is held between the chair and Strathclyde Pre-school Playgroups Association. The regional pre-five development officer meets regularly with voluntary sector personnel. At headquarters level, senior staff from Education and Social Work meet quarterly to discuss pre-five issues. Working parties to develop policy or plan for action are also set up from time to time. At divisional level, managers in Education, Social Work and Health are in regular contact and, at a local level, as well as contact via admission panels, there will be liaison on individual issues between Education, Social Work and Health staff.

Thus a variety of formal and informal groups existed which could be utilised to take forward policy development and to promote effective practice. Ideas and concerns of relevance to registration issues, quality of service issues and development in the future were being shared in advance of both the draft guidance and the Act itself. The region had also recently conducted an extensive survey of 1,000 parents of children under five which provided an overview of their circumstances, priorities and preferences for different types of services. The findings, which were the result of work done in 1988, provided useful background material to put alongside information emerging from the Children Act consultations.

Getting Started on the Review of Services

The Regional Council formally adopted the Education (Pre-Five) Sub-Committee as the advisory body which set the terms of reference and approved the procedures for the conduct of the Review, and, following wide consultation on draft reports, approved the final reports on its outcome. Officers of other departments of the regional council, such as the Chief Executive's Department and Social Work, officers and members of the Voluntary Sector Forum in Strathclyde and officers of the Health Boards also had the opportunity to influence the conduct of the Review, through their representation on the pre-five committee. Reference has already been made to the working parties established in Spring 1991, to advise on procedures to be adopted for the regulation of daycare and childminding services for under eights and on the nature and conduct of the Review. Regional councillors did not have day to day involvement in the work of these groups but were kept advised of progress being made, formally through reports to committee and at periodic briefing meetings, for the chair of the pre-five committee, for example.

The working parties brought together regional council staff, including officers from Pre-Five Services, Community Education, Social Work and Legal Services. Voluntary sector representatives in the working parties included, for example, volunteers and/or staff from the Strathclyde Pre-school Play Association, Strathclyde Childminding Association, Strathclyde Playscheme Working Party and Stepping Stones in Scotland. Contact was established with English associations which represented the private sector in an effort to establish contact with an umbrella organisation which could represent private nursery owners in Strathclyde. No such organisation existed at that time, however. The private sector was not, therefore, represented in the working parties but individual private nursery owners were consulted on the draft Review reports. Liaison has since been established between pre-five services and the newly formed West of Scotland Branch of the Scottish Independent Nurseries Association.

Review Process

Because of the size of Strathclyde Region, in terms of population and geography, it was decided that the Review should be conducted within each of the six existing educational divisions, together with a region wide overview. Seven booklets on the Review were therefore produced which, taken together, form Strathclyde Region's Review of Services.

The overall strategy for the conduct of the Review was co-ordinated by pre-five headquarters staff, guided by advice from the working party. The strategy was agreed by Education Officers with responsibility for pre-five services in divisions and confirmed by the Pre-Five Sub-Committee. Divisional staff conducted the Review in their own area, following the plan adopted, and headquarters staff produced the regional report.

The table Fig. 2.4, (on page 28) gives an outline of the review process in Strathclyde.

Key features of the strategy adopted for the Review were:

- Presentation of reports to committees
- Initial data collation
- Production of draft reports
- Consultation on draft reports, and revision and production of the final reports

Each of these features are now considered briefly.

Figure no. 2.4 Summary of review process in Strathclyde Region

Date	Departmental Briefing Papers Title and Purpose		Reports to Pre 5 Committee Title and Purpose		Data Collation	Consultation
March 1991	Comments on and response to draft guidance on the Children Act.	To examine in detail the implications of the draft guidelines issued by the Scottish Office			Register constantly updated.	Ongoing liaison with the voluntary sector forum, Social Work Department and Health Boards, through the activities of the working parties formed to establish registration and review procedures and through liaison structures already established.
June 1991		The Children Act staffing resource.	To advise committee of new duties conferred by the Act, including the conduct of the review.			
February 1992			The Children Act 1989.	To advise committee on progress being made in implementing the Act. To advise that detailed papers on the review duty would follow.	Re-registration exercise brought the register more up to date.	
April 1992	Draft Review and consultation process.	To establish the basis of the review.				
May 1992	Collation of basic data.	To identify the range of data to be collated and to identify its source.				
May 1992	Outline structure of initial divisional review booklets.	To agree an initital structure for review reports.	The Children Act, 1989 Review of Services	To name the lead officer, establish the advisory review committee and agree the content and structure of the review.		
May 1992	Action Note.	To inform Education Officers and Development Officers of action to be taken.				
July 1992	Structure of Review Booklets	To finalise structure of the draft documents			— Computerised data programme designed. Registrered persons lists updated. Organisations asked to inform region of registrable and exempt support services.	— Meetins with Voluntary Sector Forum to plan consultation with Voluntary Sector.
August 1992			The Children Act 1992, consultation process.	To establish the consultation process.	Inputting of data on needs and resources. Writing of draft reports.	— meetings with social work staff on social work input to review.
October/ November 1992	1. Response to draft booklets. 2. Review: Next Steps. 3. Revision of draft documents.	To brief staff on the processes to be adopted for consultation and revision	Regional Report on Service to under 8s.	To make a presentation to Pre 5 Committee on the draft review. Booklets approved for consultation		Issue of consultation documents, — Briefing/consultation meetings with Pre 5 staff and other interested parties.
December 1992 to January 1993					Revision of draft documents. Updating data on needs and resources.	— Collation of 419 written responses and summaries of consultation meetings.
February 1993	The Way Ahead.	To outline possible future policy and service developments. For discussion at a senior management and political level.				
March 1993			The Children Act 1989, Review of Childminding, Daycare and Education Services for Children under 8.	The completed review of services for approval by committee and by the council.		Copies of final reports on the review were widely circulated.

Presentation of reports to committee

The department briefing papers which were produced, listed in Fig 2.4, established the content of the reports which were presented to committee. The Education (Pre-Five) Sub Committee, as indicated earlier, set the terms of reference for the Review and approved the procedures for its conduct by discussing and approving these reports.

The Committee, during this period, also considered and approved detailed reports on the regulation of childminding and daycare services for children under eight and approved the standards and procedures adopted in Strathclyde for registration and inspection of these services.

Initial data collation

Basic information on registered services existing in Strathclyde was taken from the register which was current at the time (June 1992). Information on playschemes and out of school care schemes held on the register was incomplete as many of these services had not been registered. By consulting with, for example, supporting organisations and bodies like Strathclyde After School Care Association and the Playscheme Working Party, the numbers of these groups were established. Details of services provided by the Education Department were collated from internal department sources. The Social Work Department, District Councils, Health Boards, independent schools, prisons and HM Forces establishments were asked to provide information on daycare, supervised activities and supportive services they provided for under eights.

Demographic information on the under eight population was collated on a regional, divisional and postcode district basis. Figures which demonstrated the levels of various types of provision were also gathered. Indicators of need were chosen to reflect the council's concern to make services available, in the first instance, to vulnerable children. The range of indicators used was limited by the decision to provide information on a postcode district basis.

These indicators were:

- the number of households with children
- the number of lone adult households with children
- the number of births to mothers under 20 years old
- the number of unemployed adults in a postcode area

Postcode district areas were chosen as the building block for information as they are generally small enough to be meaningful and are easily identifiable to the public, while being large enough to enable relevant statistical information to be gathered. Difficulties did arise however because, for example, a small number of rural areas had insufficient populations to allow significant trends to be established and there were difficulties in differentiating urban and rural trends where both areas exist in one postcode district. Areas of priority treatment were not separately identifiable and information specific to rural needs, ethnic minorities and levels of children with special educational needs did not easily emerge.

However, the information gathered was usefully presented in an appendix to the divisional booklets. This provides a comprehensive list of services available in each postcode district together with the indicators of need. The task is now to regularly update this list and to refine and improve the indicators of need on which the planning of future service developments can be based.

Production of draft reports

Each draft divisional report contained an introduction which outlined the purpose of the Review, the content of the report and gave initial information on the consultation process. An analysis of population and needs was provided, followed by a divisional summary of services made available. Numbers and the role of staff providing services to under eights, in the Education and Social Work Departments were given, together with details of staff development programmes. Support given to and the part played by the private and voluntary sectors was featured in the reports, which concluded by examining possible proposals for the further development of the service.

The region wide report brought together the main features of the divisional reports, compared and contrasted divisional needs and resources, set out the relevant policies of the Council and discussed possible policy options for the future development of the service.

Consultation on draft reports

Informal consultation on the Review took place with Social Work, Health Boards and voluntary organisations, at regional and divisional level, prior to the production of the draft Review. Draft reports were approved as consultation documents by the Education (Pre-Five) Sub-Committee on 6 October 1992 and, thereafter, the reports were issued for consultation. The Glasgow divisional report was translated into the six main ethnic languages.

Advertisements were placed in two national newspapers and local newspapers across the region advising that copies of the reports were available from headquarters and divisional offices. A proforma was issued with each copy of the report asking for comments on its content. A closing date of 4 December was set for submission of comments. It was generally believed, by the authority and by others involved in the process, that the timescale laid down for consultation was much too short. However, despite the restrictions which this timescale imposed, the reports were made available and a series of consultation meetings were held.

Copies of the draft regional report together with the appropriate divisional report(s) were issued to:

- all regional councillors
- all pre-five establishments
- Social Work Department, at regional and district levels
- district councils
- libraries
- community councils
- Voluntary Sector Forum
- voluntary organisations, such as the Scottish Pre-school Play Association and the Scottish Childminding Association
- Link-up groups
- National Association of Local Government Officers
- Educational Institute for Scotland
- Professional Association of Teachers
- National Association of School Masters/Union of Women Teachers
- National Union of Public Employees
- Association of Head Teachers
- Advisory Group on Women's Issues
- Scottish Parent Teacher Council
- Strathclyde School Parents Federation
- Strathclyde Community Relations Council
- Advisory Committee on Racial Equality

In total 10,000 draft reports were produced for distribution throughout the region at a cost of £25,000 to the Council.

Consultation meetings were held at regional, divisional and local level. One of the main planks of consultation at regional level was a meeting held with the Voluntary Sector Forum on 26 October 1992: 36 representatives of voluntary organisations with an interest in services for under eights and their families attended and a summary of the proceedings was produced.

Arrangements for consultation at and within divisions varied and included:

- at divisional level – presentations made to divisional community development committees, open meetings and consultation with Health Boards, Social Work, psychological services, Community Education, voluntary organisations, parents and private sector providers.
- at local level –   open meetings and consultations with voluntary organisations, social work, pre-five staff, members of school boards, parents and Link-Up groups.

At total of 92 consultation meetings were held throughout the region; 419 written submissions were received on the draft reports.

Revision

The final reports on the Review were written in the light of comments received on the draft reports. These comments included opinions on the possible future development of services for children under eight and their families and references to possible omissions from the reports. New sections were added to each report, detailing the outcome of the consultation process, providing a glossary of terms, giving information on registration under the Children Act and updating useful names and addresses. In the regional report, further information on the quality and diverse nature and range of services which voluntary organisations provide was included.

Following approval by committee, copies of the regional and relevant divisional reports were made available to those individuals, organisations, establishments and groups involved in the review process. Copies were lodged in public libraries and a number were retained at regional and divisional level for staff use and for issue to enquiries. 2,500 documents were produced in the initial print run.

The work associated with the conduct of the Review was undertaken by existing regional and divisional staff. They were supported by a clerical officer appointed on a temporary basis to each division and to headquarters to collate the information. Costs were met from existing resources and staff were diverted from other activities to gather the information and to consult on and write the reports. It is recognised that the Review provided an important opportunity to conduct an audit of needs and resources, to consult on possible ways forward and to establish a sound basis for future service planning and development. It also, for a time, restricted the ability of staff involved to respond quickly, to the other ongoing management and development tasks for which they were responsible.

Implications for Future Policy and Service Development

The "Way Ahead" section of the regional report on the Review of services outlined possible ways in which the regional council could maintain and, where possible, expand and improve the quality of services for children under eight. This section re-affirmed the existing policies of the council and restated the belief that child care and education are inseparable. It confirmed the view that the child care and educational needs of young children in their early years and their families can be met through the development of joint services where provision is planned in the light of local needs and current resources. Such provision should also take into account the contribution made by the private and voluntary sectors.

From the substantial body of information and comments collected during the Review, and from other existing sources of information it is clear that there is an overall shortfall in provision. Unless there is a substantial shift in the level of support funding which child care and educational services attract from central government, the demand for places will continue to outstrip the supply for the foreseeable future. Against this background, the "Way Ahead" section promoted the view that a major development in the number and quality of services must be founded on an expansion of the range of active partnerships which currently exist in the region and that a variety of funding mechanisms should be considered.

These partnerships involve a range of bodies and individuals including, for example, the local authority, the voluntary sector, the private sector, employers and parents. Further to the publication of the Review, detailed consideration is being given to the policy developments and practical arrangements which are required to expand service provision and to promote quality through partnership arrangements. This development work is being given a high priority within the Education Department.

Despite the financial constraints facing the authority, it remains the policy of the council to expand departmental provision in areas of identified need, when resources become available. Areas of need were identified in each division through the review process, providing target areas for expansion when resources permit. The regional council has, since the publication of the Review, made funding available through its social strategy initiative to expand provision in the region by 315 full-time equivalent nursery places. This expansion is being achieved by developing new nurseries and by expanding the capacity of existing establishments in a small number of the areas of need. Specific proposals for other developments will be brought forward when additional resources are identified.

Comments received on the Review also identified concerns about the proposals for reorganisation of local government, expressed by many of the voluntary organisations which provide child care and educational services. Many voiced fears that the level of grant aid provided by the regional council, over £1,000,000 in year 1992/93, might not be maintained by a number of smaller authorities, resulting in a loss of service to children and families. It continues to be the policy of Strathclyde to support the voluntary sector which is recognised as making a major contribution to the provision of quality services.

Quality in services refers to both the physical environment and to the interaction that goes on between children and adults on a day to day basis. The Children Act guidance and regulations are stronger on providing standards for physical provision than for interaction. Within the Education Department the Quality Assurance Unit has produced material which gives indicators of good practice in both the physical and inter-personal environments. These indicators are backed up by exemplars of good practice. Both pre-five establishments and primary schools use the quality assurance material when auditing and reviewing their establishment's practice. The pre-five material is also available to the pre-school community organisers as information which they can use, in addition to the specific sets of standards for daycare and childminders which have been developed in the region, when discussing standards with the private and voluntary sector.

The Education Development Service has produced guidelines on a 0–5 curriculum called *Partners in Learning*. There has been consultation which has included both voluntary and primary sector. The guidelines will be available to private and voluntary sector groups and currently a shorter version of the guidelines for those coming new to the pre-five field is being produced. Staff development programmes are available to all primary and pre-five staff. It has been possible in the past to include some voluntary sector staff on courses and in the future a more comprehensive strategy will be considered to support developments under the Children Act. It would be helpful to have specific resources made available by The Scottish Office which would enable, for example, the development of distance learning packages or funding of the Scottish Vocational Qualification for workers in child care and education in the voluntary sector.

Towards the next review

A number of lessons can be learned from the conduct of the first Review of services which, if fully considered, could contribute to ensuring that the next Review is conducted more effectively. At a national level there should be a common framework for collating information on needs and resources. It would be helpful if agreement could be reached, for example, on the core information which should be contained in future reports and on the terminology which is used to describe service provision. Reaching agreement on these matters will be a complicated task but is necessary if a proper analysis and comparison of the information produced by regions is to be made.

The guidance on the conduct of the Review which was issued by The Scottish Office contained an expectation that qualitative as well as quantitative information was to be provided. Further debate at a national level on what qualitative information is to be contained in future reports and how it might be effectively gathered is needed. The adequacy of the resources made available to local authorities to conduct the Review also requires to be considered at a national level.

Planning for the conduct of the next Review is beginning in Strathclyde. This will build on the database which has been established but will reflect any movement made at a national level to establish a common information base. Consideration will be given to the means of updating the information gathered in the first Review, perhaps on an annual basis, and to the means of resourcing and conducting this work. Such work will continue to be founded on liaison and collaboration with others having an interest in the provision of education and caring services for children under eight.

TAYSIDE REGION
Ros Kirk, Principal Officer, Children and Young People

This chapter aims to put the implementation of the Children Act in Tayside within its wider national and local context. It focuses on the progress of the work between the Social Work and Education Departments through the developing roles of key officers and the new structures which they set up in response to the Act.

The background to the Review in Tayside

In addition to the limitations surrounding the Children Act legislation itself, further understanding of the management and extent of change brought about by the Children Act in Tayside requires some consideration of other contextual factors including other demands on resources, the nature of the Region and the range of early years services which were available in the period leading up to the Children Act. All of these wider aspects influenced the way implementation took place.

The legislative context

At the turn of the decade, in common with all other local authorities, Tayside Regional Council was responding at an unprecedented rate to a wide range of changes to the law relating to local government roles and responsibilities, including methods of calculating, collecting and distributing the finance of local government itself.

The Social Work Department, in partnership with the Health Board and others, was negotiating and implementing radical reform to the planning and delivery of services to the elderly and those with disabilities under the NHS and Community Care Act 1990. Social Work services to offenders were also subject to change to such an extent that reorganisation was necessary at both national and local levels. The delivery of children's services retained some degree of relative stability at this time, although sweeping changes were anticipated in a forthcoming White Paper on Scottish Child Care Law, which, it was hoped, would integrate recommendations resulting from national reviews of child, family and adoption law, major public inquiries and the Children Act Part X and Section 19. There was growing public debate about the role and effectiveness of social work in the lives of children and their parents and it was hoped that new legislation of the kind anticipated would provide an opportunity to address some of these issues.

The Education Department was also under considerable pressure managing the introduction of national testing, devolved school management, extensive changes to the delivery and planning of the curriculum across all age groups and a new staff development and review programme.

The local political context

Tayside Regional Council had a finely balanced small Labour majority, making it all the more necessary to ensure that politicians were kept fully advised of forthcoming proposals which had resource implications whilst recognising that elected members could easily become overloaded with information about new duties and responsibilities from various Departments. The climate was a turbulent one in which demands for finite resources were high. The Children Act had to take its place in the queue.

The local demographic and socio-economic context

Tayside is the fourth largest Scottish Regional and Islands Authority both in population and area accounting for 7.7% of the country's population and covering some 2,897 square miles. In mid-1991, there were an estimated 392,500 people in Tayside, within local district council areas: Dundee (172,400) Perth and Kinross (124,850) and Angus (92,250). Children under eight years of age comprised almost 10% of the Region's population (38,000) (General Register Office, Scotland).

According to the latest national Census in 1991, the proportion of households in Tayside with one or more dependent children was 28% (Scotland average 30%). Over 18% of children aged 0–4 years were in lone parent households. In Dundee this rose to almost 27% (more than one child in four). There were a total of 7,386 lone parents in the Region, over 60% of them in Dundee. The percentage of ethnic minority residents in Tayside (1.2%) was similar to the national average, although this varied from 0.5% in Angus to 2% in Dundee. In 1992 the Scottish Low Pay Unit reported that all groups of workers in Tayside had earnings below the national average. (Payline, 14)

The Need for Daycare in Tayside

As in the rest of Scotland, Tayside has experienced an increase in the number of women entering the labour market in recent years, despite an unemployment rate of around 11% in 1993 (Department of Employment). The rise in female employment rates has generally been within part-time, lower paid jobs. As a result of the working patterns and hours, many of the women find themselves unprotected in terms of statutory employment rights such as sick leave entitlement and maternity benefits. Access to high quality, affordable daycare is therefore of particular importance to those on low incomes who wish to work and improve their quality of life (Brown and Tait, 1992). The majority of parents in Scotland rely on informal arrangements, usually with relatives to care for their children when working (Cohen, 1992).

Parents use early years provision for many different reasons. It provides social and educational experiences for young children and broad supportive functions to the family. It may enable parents to work, take up further education or training, develop skills, make new friends, participate in the wider community or give increased access to social support. As a result of the fragmented origins of services there is a tendency for them to become segregated according to their primary function as defined by the management agencies and ultimately by levels of parental income. Despite differing reasons for use, all children should experience high-quality care and education which stimulates and encourages development. Research and debate about quality has grown rapidly in recent years (Hennessy, Martin, Moss and Melhuish, 1992). It has already been clearly demonstrated that good quality pre-school centres do enhance the development of young children and increase educational attainment and social adjustment into adulthood (Sylvia 1992). The national case for widespread access to daycare has been made for some time.

It was evident to those living and working in Tayside that the national situation was reflected locally, with variations in availability related to geography and the cost of services.

Daycare in Tayside before the Children Act

A tradition of providing some public daycare for working women existed in Dundee, dating back to the previous century. Historical and economic influences arising from the city's dependence on a largely female workforce in the jute mills of the 19th century and early 20th century resulted in four times the amount of public daycare places than elsewhere in the Region today. (Four full-time equivalent places for every hundred children under five in Dundee with less than one place per hundred elsewhere (Tayside Regional Council, 1993)). Education Department and private nurseries also thrived in Dundee in response to the same political and historical forces which affect public daycare. In earlier days women were often the main breadwinners in working-class Dundonian families who supported both their families and the industries which depended upon their cheap labour.

Although Dundee also developed other types of services, such as playgroups and childminders, these tended to supplement informal care arrangements and core public services, whereas other parts of Tayside were more reliant on voluntary and private sector efforts to back up the informal arrangements parents made.

The Regional Council consistently invested over the five years up to and including the year of implementation in expanding and refurbishing existing daycare and education services for young children with a number of new Social Work child and family centres and Education nursery schools and classes opened. Attempts were being made to redress the geographical anomalies by opening up pre-school centres in rural areas which previously had no public services.

A large number of departments and agencies had responsibility for, or become involved in, a number of statutory and non-statutory services at a national as well as local level:

- Regulation of childminding, playgroups and private nurseries
- Support and training
- Provision of early years daycare, education and family support services
- Creche provision
- Out of School and holiday playschemes .

Evidence of a collaborative approach to the development of early years provision dates back to 1981 when the Region's first joint Social Work and Education pre-school centre was opened in Perth. Since then, other models have been developed, experimenting with partnerships involving voluntary organisations and, on two occasions, the Health Board. Urban Aid funding was used to initiate a number of innovative joint projects, including a community business daycare venture. Voluntary organisations such as the Aberlour Child Care Trust, YMCA, Scottish Council for Single Parents, Fair Play and the Scottish Pre-school Play Association positively contributed to the range and support of early years services in the Region. The provision of public services in Tayside was further influenced by Regional policies to target areas of social priority for resource allocation.

Accurate, up to date information about services was not readily available from a single source. Parents seeking daycare for their child were therefore required to undertake an individual exercise of collating information from various sources and combining this with any informal arrangements which were required to best meet the needs of their families. The situation was far from ideal, depending as it did on individual parent's skills and knowledge as well as their support networks.

The Children Act was not the beginning of collaboration in, and concern for, increased early years provision in Tayside. It did, however, add impetus and urgency to adopt a more co-ordinated approach in the absence of any structures which could facilitate this.

Preparation for Implementation

Inter-Agency Working Group to respond to The Scottish Office Draft Guidance, December 1991

Between Christmas and New Year of 1990, The Scottish Office issued draft guidance on the Act to local authorities. A three-month period was available for a response to be prepared. As it was recognised that the amount of preparation which would be required to respond to the new legislative requirements would be substantial, given the numbers of agencies and departments involved, it was seen as essential in Tayside to begin to frame the work as early as possible. To this end, the Social Work Department set up and chaired a cross sector working group to prepare a corporate response to the guidance. It was thought important to inform as many interested agencies and groups as possible and invite their participation and therefore copies of the draft guidance were widely circulated to individuals and groups. In the event, sixteen representatives attended the working group meetings with others commenting in other ways. This was the beginning of establishing consultation mechanisms to support implementation. There was enthusiasm amongst the group members to give detailed and serious thought to the task. The meetings were topic based and programmed to enable members to be selective if they so wished and to prepare appropriately beforehand.

A response document was drawn up highlighting the implications of the new duties and responsibilities and raising a number of points which required further clarification. Concern and anger was expressed about the brief implementation timescale, compounded by the absence of specific, additional finance. It was bewildering that the information to be prepared by local authorities was not wanted for any purposes by central government. Comment was also made about the inconsistencies in regulation which covered some child care services but exempted others, such as babysitting organisations and most nannying arrangements in which young children could be equally vulnerable.

The response was formally supported at a political level by both the Social Work and Education Committees before it went to The Scottish Office. It was important to bring this quickly into the political domain by taking the response to the Committees. It did, however, reduce the amount of time available for wider consultation.

Although it is recognised that membership and consultation was limited the short lived inter-agency working group was a useful way of bringing departments and sectors together in a task centred and purposeful way. It served to raise initial awareness of forthcoming changes and attempted to reach representatives of various interested parties. It demonstrated the intention of the Council to be open, work in partnership and formed the basis for future consultation. It would also have been useful to have made it an explicit task of group members to disseminate the work of the group within their own agency with progress on this made a standing item on the agenda. The introduction of change, particularly if it is centrally driven, requires to be widely discussed at an early stage to avoid those who are to be directly affected feeling remote from decision making, resistant and powerless.

The report to Social Work and Education Committees provided opportunities to raise political awareness of the proposed legislative changes and the likely need for additional resources in the near future.

Joint Report to Social Work, Education and Personnel Committees in response to the final Scottish Office Guidance, June 1992

A period of three months followed without any further word from The Scottish Office until June when the final guidance document was issued. No substantive changes had been made. It was at this point that the authority began to place growing importance upon the forthcoming changes with increased involvement from politicians and chief officers.

The earlier groundwork proved worthwhile enabling a coherent argument to be made for additional resources and new co-ordination structures to be put relatively quickly to the Social Work, Education and Personnel Committees and ultimately to the Policy and Resources Committee. Speed was important given that only three months had been given from the issue of guidance to the date of implementation.

The joint report outlined the following shared concerns which needed to be addressed:

- Low levels of all types of daycare provision
- Inadequacy of information about services
- Lack of co-ordination and consultation with parents
- Future development of joint provision while recognising the distinctive contributions made by Departments and sectors
- Inequality of opportunity arising from availability and access

Proposals were made to address these issues:
1. Through creating structures for co-ordination and consultation and to make policy more informed (see diagram), including
   - a Regional Under Eights Co-ordinating Group, comprising members of both Committees
   - a widely representative cross sector regional working group to support the work of the Co-ordinating Group
   - the development of Under Eights Consultation Fora at district level to improve local consultation and co-ordination

Diagram 1. Regional and District Structures for the Co-ordination of Services for the Under Eights.

POLICY AND PLANNING

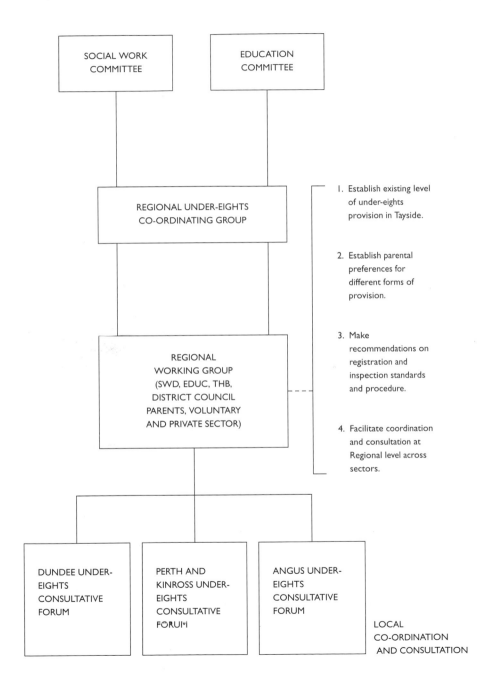

SOCIAL WORK COMMITTEE

EDUCATION COMMITTEE

REGIONAL UNDER-EIGHTS CO-ORDINATING GROUP

REGIONAL WORKING GROUP (SWD, EDUC, THB, DISTRICT COUNCIL PARENTS, VOLUNTARY AND PRIVATE SECTOR)

1. Establish existing level of under-eights provision in Tayside.

2. Establish parental preferences for different forms of provision.

3. Make recommendations on registration and inspection standards and procedure.

4. Facilitate coordination and consultation at Regional level across sectors.

DUNDEE UNDER-EIGHTS CONSULTATIVE FORUM

PERTH AND KINROSS UNDER-EIGHTS CONSULTATIVE FORUM

ANGUS UNDER-EIGHTS CONSULTATIVE FORUM

LOCAL CO-ORDINATION AND CONSULTATION

2. To ensure that a partnership approach between Social Work and Education underpinned work related to the Children Act

- by setting up an Inter-Departmental Advisory Group to bring together key officers with responsibilities for the Children Act to oversee implementation
- through the appointment of mirror Development Officer posts in both departments to undertake the primary Review tasks
- by appointing a Training Co-ordinator to work alongside the Social Work Training Officer to develop training in this area
- by appointing the same amount of clerical support in each department to support the review and training work
- by creating new registration officers
- by viewing consultation on childminding and daycare standards as a high priority
- by creating small, matching budgets for publications, training and research
- by creating a small Social Work budget to enable wider consultation with other sectors on the implications of the Act

The preparation of this joint report was instrumental in breaking down further some of the departmental boundaries surrounding early years provision. It provided a focus for agreeing and clarifying the issues of common concern and made commitment to a joint plan of action to address these.

The financial and practice implications were greater for Social Work than for the Education Department because of the changes to regulation duties. The total cost to the Region was a quarter of a million pounds with four-fifths of this required by Social Work. To secure this extent of additional funding required a confident and secure political base backed by sound professional advice. Support and informed appreciation of the issues from the Conveners of both Committees was essential. It was their task to convince other elected members in a Council with a small majority that money spent on daycare would be advantageous to their constituents and that it should be given relatively high priority in comparison to other needs within the Region.

The Scottish Office had still not requested copies of the Review reports produced by local authorities. This demonstrated a continuing reluctance to view child care as a national issue and indicated that the Review was a relatively low priority in relation to other areas. It required lobbying by individual authorities, the Association of Directors of Social Work and Children in Scotland (then SCAFA) amongst others to change this and an instruction to eventually be issued requiring Review reports to be sent to The Scottish Office by 31 March 1992.

Implementation – 14 October 1991

From the time that additional resources were made available the experience of joint work between the Education and Social Work Departments became qualitatively different. The Directors clearly gave the work a very high priority, always giving it space on inter-departmental joint directorate agendas and expecting high commitment and standards from the lead officers.

The Interdepartmental Advisory Group

The lead officers who had been identified by the Directors were at a senior level within both departments, namely the Assistant Director of Education (0–10), the Education Nursery Adviser and the Principal Officer (Children and Young People) in the Social Work Department. These officers formed the core of the inter-departmental Advisory Group which soon expanded to include the Head of Inspection, Quality Assurance Unit, Social Work Department and the Principal Officer (Community Education). As the newly appointed Development Officers and Training Co-ordinator came into post they formed the Review Team with responsibility for undertaking the work of the Review on a day to day basis. They also participated in the Advisory Group along with a Training Officer from Social Work.

As the group increased in size the remit also grew increasingly complex. The remit included:

- the development and implementation of an information and publicity strategy
- staff appointment, training and management
- the method and content of the Review report
- the support and establishment of regional and local consultation and co-ordination structures
- the development and implementation of a consultation strategy
- discussion of the standards to be applied in childminding and daycare for the under eights

The breadth of the agenda required frequent meetings to enable consensus decision making to be reached. The group dynamics were challenging, at times highly productive and frustrating at others. It was experienced as both stressful and supportive to those involved at various points. A considerable amount of time and energy was put into building relationships, role clarification and reaching mutual understanding. As implementation progressed the amount of time and energy committed added to the experience of shared responsibility and for the work to be truly joint. This was unrealistic in terms of time and energy in the longer term but did help create a truly shared basis for future inter-departmental early years work.

Diagram 2.

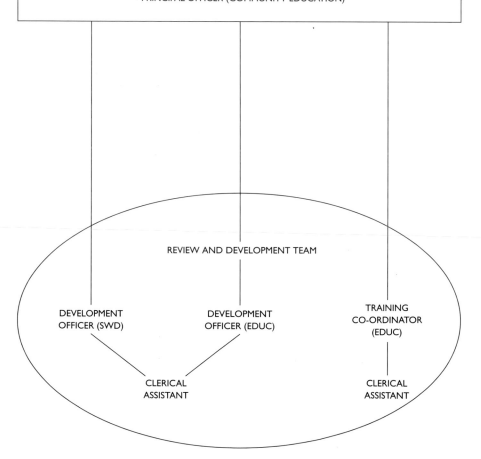

INTER-DEPARTMENTAL ADVISORY GROUP

SWD:- PRINCIPAL OFFICER,
(CHILDREN AND YOUNG PEOPLE)

• TRAINING OFFICER,

• HEAD OF REGISTRATION

EDUC:- ASSISTANT DIRECTOR,

• ADVISER IN NURSERY EDUCATION,

• PRINCIPAL OFFICER (COMMUNITY EDUCATION)

REVIEW AND DEVELOPMENT TEAM

DEVELOPMENT
OFFICER (SWD)

DEVELOPMENT
OFFICER (EDUC)

TRAINING
CO-ORDINATOR
(EDUC)

CLERICAL
ASSISTANT

CLERICAL
ASSISTANT

To manage the tasks it soon became evident that operational management was becoming confused with management being the shared responsibility of the Assistant Director of Education, the Principal Officer (Social Work) and the Education Nursery Adviser who formed a small Management Group. Unavoidable changes in training officer personnel at this time affected the extent to which training issues became fully integrated into the review process.

The management of any change requires a small number of key individuals to innovate and create new ways of doing things, taking risks and responsibility for seeing things through. There should be continuity within the group wherever possible to avoid fragmentation. Conflict needs to be managed to avoid it becoming destructive. This may be through open discussion and reaching joint agreement on how to progress. This may not always be possible and compromises may have to be made and changes to plans made accordingly. It may also be necessary, as a last resort, to exert authority to ensure that agreed tasks and timescales are met. There will need to be flexibility about roles and responsibilities. Inter-departmental work is dependent on mutual respect and trust developing between the key officers. This takes time and commitment, particularly in the early stages. It is undoubtedly worthwhile in terms of ready access to a wider range of skills, knowledge and resources. The foundation and a possible model for future joint work is also established.

It had originally been hoped to include representatives from other sectors in the inter-departmental advisory group but this did not happen for pragmatic reasons. This would probably have created another dimension of complexity to the purposes and working of this group. Their absence however detracted from the open, equal partnership approach which had been intended. Implementation was then driven by the interests of the two lead Departments rather than other providers or parents. It was hoped that the establishment of the other co-ordination and consultation structures might counterbalance this.

The review team and joint training

Although this stage clearly overlaps with the development of the Advisory Group the recruitment, appointment and training of the Review Team was done on a partnership basis under its direction.

Although this was time consuming it was valuable as it provided further opportunities for key officers to share responsibility for staff selection and any subsequent consequences which arose. It was necessary for the key officers to agree explicitly on the qualifications, skills and experience required for each of the different posts and this meant that together they had to explore and reach common agreement about roles, responsibilities and expectations of the Review. As no previous model of Review work was available there was a tendency to focus on the most tangible task of producing a comprehensive Review report.

When all new and existing officers responsible for implementing regulation and review duties under the Act were in post, an intensive three-day residential training programme was organised and provided by the Social Work Department as most of the participants were employed by them. The training aimed to develop skills, awareness of new roles and responsibilities and to build teams which were inter-related and inter-dependent. The inter-departmental context was reinforced by the Directors of Social Work and Education who attended to introduce events on alternate days.

Lead officers had carried so much personal responsibility for carrying out tasks associated with the Act while remaining responsible for other work that there was considerable pressure on the newly appointed Review Team to be able to pick up and run with their new jobs. Expectations were high and time was very short. The complex and lengthy Advisory Group agendas and the involvement of the Review team may have assisted with clarification of roles and responsibilities. Review team members were having to adjust to their appointments in newly created promoted posts, based at the centre of the organisation. They had to adjust to the political nature of their work, acquire new skills and knowledge very quickly and to negotiate new professional relationships at all levels. On this foundation they had to publish a draft report eight or nine months after taking up post.

A partnership approach to staffing is fundamental to joint working. It openly demonstrates commitment and acknowledges the contribution to be made by others. Responsibility is further shared when management issues arise. It provides further opportunities for focused discussion about the work and ways of managing it. This increases mutual understanding and helps trust to develop between key officers. It can also, however, add complexity to working relationships when lines of accountability become more diffuse. It is more time consuming than the exclusive, hierarchical approach but the rewards are potentially far greater.

Similarly, a joint training strategy is essential as a means of enabling the development of mutual understanding at an operational as well as policy level. It is not without its practical difficulties given the different organisational structures and conditions of service of the workers involved in all types of multidisciplinary work.

Developing an Information and Publicity Strategy

Integral to the work of the Review was the collation of information and statistics about services. The lack of reliable information underpinned and potentially undermined the entire review process. Definitions of terms vary across and within agencies and between authorities. Recording was often inaccurate and maintained in various locations. Statistical comparisons which are fundamental to the task are consequently not as meaningful as they might first appear. This deteriorates further when attempts are made to build a national picture drawing on centrally collated statistics.

In the very early stages of the Review the Social Work Department responded to this by setting up a single data bank which integrated the statutory register of daycare, supplemented by all other types of daycare, education and support services for the under eights in Tayside. Local decisions were made about the definitions to be applied to different types of services but others remain unresolved. This forms the basis for the Directory of Day Care and Education Services for the Under Eights. It has been widely distributed throughout the Region and is regularly updated.

A leaflet, *Choosing the Best Care for your Child,* was published and distributed prior to the Review report to inform parents of the range of services available in Tayside. It was translated into four ethnic minority languages with the distinctive design being carried through in further publications on daycare.

A range of activities was also used to publicise changes, seek views and information. These included using the media to issue press releases and place adverts. Staff briefings and public meetings were also held at various times. Letters and questionnaires to providers were distributed widely. Ultimately the draft Review report itself was used as focus for consultation. Nine public consultation meetings were held in various locations throughout the Region. One thousand people commented in the course of the review process. In addition, the formal structures set up in response to the Act were also used. All of these initiatives were jointly planned and carried out.

A joint, comprehensive information, publicity and consultation strategy is crucial to the review process. There was a tendency this time to respond to issues as they arose but greater awareness of these will inform the next Review. These were always discussed at the Advisory Group who shared responsibility, although one or other Department needed to take the lead on each initiative, otherwise confusion arose.

There is an urgent need for improved information systems based on nationally agreed indicators and measures of services provision. This is a complex task which requires national and local collaboration as early as possible to ensure that levels patterns and range of services can be accurately and reliably compared across the country.

Political Involvement – The Regional Under Eights Co-ordinating Group

Political involvement primarily took place within the formal settings of the Social Work and Education Committees and the Regional Under Eights Group which provided opportunity for them to consider Children Act issues in more detail prior to discussion at full Committees. It was chaired on an annual rotating basis by the Convener of Social Work and the Convener of Education with membership drawn from both Committees, totalling six elected members with officers from the Departments of Social Work and Education in attendance. The administration of the group was provided by the Department of Law and Administration. The status of the group within the Council fell short of that of Sub-Committee. It was therefore small enough for meaningful discussion but not properly constituted to avoid the necessity of reports going to full Committees as well. As timescales for the Review were very short it was not always possible to present material first to the Co-ordinating Group and involve elected members to the extent which had been envisaged. The Co-ordinating Group met only once in the year following implementation.

The establishment of a joint political structure to exclusively consider early years issues was of significant symbolic importance and potential benefit to a co-ordinated approach to service planning in this area. However, the status of the group tended to duplicate time and effort for politicians and officers alike. Full advantage was not taken of elected members' willingness to be involved and might have been different had they been unhappy with the progress and direction being taken.

The demands of developing effective inter-departmental and cross-sector structures as well as undertaking other everyday tasks resulting from the Act took priority when time was of the essence.

The Cross-Sector Group – the Regional Under Eights Working Group

Following the meeting of the Co-ordinating Group in January 1992, the Regional Working Group was established to be representative of providers from all sectors, parents, ethnic minority groups and those concerned with provision for children with special needs. By definition this group was large and diverse with over thirty members. Its purpose was to undertake more detailed work in sub-groups to establish existing levels of provision, parental preferences, make recommendations on daycare and childminding standards and to facilitate regional co-ordination and consultation. This group was also supported, administratively, by the Department of Law and Administration and, professionally, by the key officers. For this group to work effectively it required to meet frequently or to be active within sub-groups. It was a structure which gave opportunity for new relationships between representatives of a wide range of interests to be forged and provide new and creative forces for change. However, it takes energy and commitment to reach this stage. Many of the members of the group were struggling to manage implementation as it affected their everyday responsibilities, while others viewed the Children Act as peripheral to their main concerns. The work of the group required the impetus of the publication of the Review report to give focus to activity.

A regional structure must offer an effective method of co-ordination and consultation which incorporates a wide range of interests, including parents. For this to be truly effective the amount of support and training this involves should not be underestimated as the aim is to achieve agreed aims and objectives for early years policy from a group comprising individuals with very different and frequently conflicting interests. It was not possible in the first year of implementation to devote this extent of resource input. It had been hoped that this group would assist in the dissemination of information about the Review and help to set up the local consultation forum. This was achieved to a very limited extent but some very useful work was undertaken by sub-groups on issues raised by the Review.

Given the demands on time and resources it might have been more appropriate to establish this group after the Review report was published although this would have restricted the extent of consultation on its contents.

Local Co-ordination and Consultation – District Forum

It was not until two years after implementation that a District Forum in each of the three districts, first outlined in the joint Committee report of 1991, began to take shape. Personnel and small amounts of financial support were not available until this time and resulted from reviewing the way resources were allocated at the time of implementation.

The development of District Fora may be critical to the success of the consultation and co-ordination strategy in Tayside as they have the potential to influence all other structures locally and regionally.

It has become evident that moving towards an integrated policy and planning process based on wide consultation is a lengthy process. It will not work unless those who are to be involved understand the way a large organisation like the Regional Council operates. Wider participation depends on adequate levels of support, membership, within groups, of key individuals who will take responsibility for effecting change. It is too early to say how effective these district groups might be. They may be vulnerable to lack of clarity of purpose or have insufficient access to resources. It was never intended that change be imposed from the top down. It should ideally result from dynamic interaction between groups which influence and shape each other. The structures which have been set up should therefore be responsive to change but must retain sufficient stability for ideas to be carried through. It may be appropriate at this time to devote further resources (including joint training) to support the achievement of both short- and long-term goals identified by the District Forum.

Summary of key lessons from this Review

- Full consideration must be given to the wider context.
- Political involvement should be supported and encouraged.

- A small number of key officers should develop inter-agency work based on mutual respect and clearly identified, shared goals and objectives.
- Key officers should share responsibility for developing and implementing an information, publicity and consultation strategy.
- Key officers should share responsibility for staff recruitment and support.
- The development of daycare standards should be done collaboratively between departments, other sectors and parents.
- A joint training strategy is essential.
- Structures should be reviewed to ensure they promote effective co-ordination, consultation and planning; flexibility should be retained.
- More effort must be made to involve those representing wide interests including parents and other sectors, in all aspects of the Review.
- Contribution must be made to the national and local debate about daycare levels and quality.
- Successful models of joint working should be adopted in other areas of work.

Outcome of the Review in Tayside

A number of positive outcomes have resulted from the Review which affect resource levels and future inter-departmental work. It was recognised that there was an on-going role for an inter-departmental advisory group following publication of the Review report and this is now established. Its remit and development plan has been agreed by the joint directorate covering the Review structures for co-ordination and consultation, research and information, training, quality assurance, issues raised by consultation on the Review report and preparation for the next Review.

Additional resources have been made available by both departments. The Education Department is providing more places in nursery classes and increased funding to playgroups for 1993–94. The Social Work Department has created new posts in both rural districts to support District Forum and increase the level and quality of daycare. Small sums of money have been allocated to each Forum to further this support.

Both departments have been involved in the preparation and delivery of induction training for playgroup leaders and childminders. Training on the assessment of daycare standards was provided by an external consultant and a number of other training events on registration and equal opportunities have taken place. Standards for the registration of childminders and daycare providers are being reviewed and up-dated. A number of information leaflets on different aspects of daycare are being prepared. Brief summary reports and leaflets on the Review have been published.

Other issues identified by the Review are now the subject of detailed consideration by the Regional Working Group, including the need for services for the under twos and services for children after school and in school holidays. The group is also looking at the use of services by children with special needs and families from ethnic minorities.

Independent research had been conducted on the use and quality of Social Work Department Child and Family Centres. A longitudinal study is also underway contrasting parental and child outcomes associated with family support linked to different public service models of early years provision. A study on parental preferences is also under consideration.

A new data base has been set up to inform a widely available directory of childminding, daycare and support services for children under eight. Awareness has been heightened of the inadequacies of current information systems and gaps in crucial information for the planning of services. Resolution will, however, be more complex and will involve national discussion.

It must be borne in mind that it has taken centuries to reach the current position in which daycare finds itself. It is unrealistic to expect that local authorities alone, responding to this piece of legislation, can radically alter the levels and patterns of daycare in Scotland without central policy direction and co-ordination alongside considerable increases in resources. It is also important that this piece of legislation is integrated into the wider proposed legal changes in all other aspects of child care.

Forthcoming reorganisation of local government will add a further challenge to ensuring that children and families are afforded equal opportunities through the provision of high-quality daycare. The wider context of daycare in Scotland will be to the fore in the next Review and must be used positively to benefit Scotland's future generations.

HIGHLAND REGION
Carole Taylor, Regional Review Co-ordinator

Early in August 1992 I took up my position as Day Care Co-ordinator in the Children's Resource Section of the Social Work Department. As an additional worker to the Section, it was considered appropriate to assign me the task of co-ordinating the review of daycare provision for children under eight years of age.

Although I had transferred from another section of the same Department I had not had direct involvement with daycare provision other than with my clients who were consumers of the service. My immediate priority therefore was to aquaint myself with the Children Act 1989, Part X and Section 19 in particular, and also the guidance provided by The Scottish Office. Having digested as much of this information as was possible within the time limits imposed on me, I was feeling rather apprehensive at the daunting prospect of having to quantify daycare and related services to the under eights in such a large geographical area with such a diverse range of demographic conditions.

The Assistant Director of Social Work had already been involved in preliminary discussions with the Education Department and the Depute Director of Education was to co-ordinate the preparation and presentation of material from his Department for the purpose of the Review. Liaison had also taken place with the Highland Scottish Pre-school Play Association regarding their contribution to the Review.

Identification

By the end of August we were examining the issues involved in tackling the Review as a whole. Time had crept up on us and we were beginning to appreciate the complexity of the tasks ahead. There were many hurdles to be overcome and the first to confront us was identification of services to be included in the Review. The actual "daycare" provision did not present any real problem because we were relatively confident it could be quite clearly identified and the Highland Scottish Pre-school Play Association were already collating the information on all the groups affiliated to their organisation.

Education Department provision was also quite clearly defined and quantifiable. Our problem arose when it came to other related services – what was a reckonable related service? The range of services which in one way or another provided for children under eight years was enormous. Should we, for example, be considering services such as grant making organisations who cater for the special needs of individual children? The list could be endless.

Organised activities presented another dilemma. How could we track down and identify every social or recreational facility which catered for children under eight years of age? We would be facing ourselves with an almost impossible and infinite task. Where were we to draw the line?

Consultation

The next issue to be resolved was that of consultation. Who did we consult and how did we consult? The main organisations involved in child care were easily contacted and consulted but how could we make the general public aware of this Review and also encourage them to participate and contribute.

Public meetings

The decision was made to hold public meetings throughout the region. Bearing in mind the limited time and manpower available and also the geography of the area, we were faced with the problem of selecting locations for these meetings. We concluded we would attempt to meet the public in each of the district council areas. These would be evening meetings in school premises based in the centres of densest population. We were very aware we were not going to reach all corners of the region and the meetings would not be accessible to all those with an interest in the Review.

The Regional Council Publicity Department was consulted and agreed to undertake the task of publicising the Review. Information on the proposed meetings was released to radio, television and newspapers serving the area. Past experiences of the Publicity Department had suggested it was counter productive to advertise too early as people then forgot about the meetings so, although general information was released in advance, the individual meetings were advertised at fairly short notice.

The local elected members of the Joint Sub-Committee were invited to chair the meetings but in most areas were unavailable to do so due to prior engagements. Senior management from both Education and Social Work Departments attended the meetings, spoke about their respective roles in the provision of services to the under eights, what was currently available and any planned future provision. They also addressed any questions or comments from the floor. Those in attendance were told this was an information gathering exercise and, although it was hoped some positive developments for future provisions would come about as a result, expectations should not be raised.

There were dissatisfactions generated in relation to the meetings. Some thought the publicity had not been adequate and sufficient notice of the meetings had not been given. The other main issue, as we had expected, was location and the inaccessibility of the meetings to many, especially those on the West Coast.

Questionnaires

A questionnaire seemed another appropriate method of gathering relevant information so we embarked on what initially appeared to be the relatively easy task of compiling a questionnaire for distribution to service providers. Trying to produce a questionnaire which is comprehensive yet concise and still user friendly when it must also have the additional quality of being computer friendly in order to facilitate data collection is anything but straightforward. However, we drew one up which, although not ideal, we felt would cover the information we were interested in and hoped to glean. Distribution was the next problem – how and to whom?

Supplies of questionnaires were made available at all the public meetings to anyone who wished to contribute. We made a direct approach to many agencies and people who we knew were involved with the provision of services to this age group but we also wanted to reach people or organisations who were not already known to us yet had a valuable contribution to make. We needed people with good local knowledge in the various districts of the Region to help us identify interested parties. Contact was made with the local Councils of Social Services who, in the main, were extremely helpful. In some areas they distributed questionnaires and also helped publicise the open meetings.

Direct contact

Direct contact was also made with organisations interested in the provision and promotion of quality daycare services to the under eights. I contacted all Social Work Teams in the Region asking for their views on the existing provision and shortfalls in services and their vision for future development of services. The response was disappointing in that I did not receive any reply at all from some teams but, at the other end of the scale, several area team leaders gave very detailed, and well researched opinions.

As already mentioned, the Assistant Director of Social Work was in contact with Highland Scottish Pre-school Play Association with regard to the collection of data relating to their organisation. I met with the Rural Tutor from the Highland Branch of the Scottish Childminding Association to discuss issues relating to Childminding provision in the Region. Comhairle Nan Sgoiltean Araich (CNSA) or the Gaelic Pre-school Council, which is one of the main providers of services to the under eights, and several of the other voluntary organisations discussed in considerable detail with me the provision they offered. Many of these organisations welcomed the opportunity to promote their service and have its value acknowledged.

Having given careful thought to the question of consultation with the Health Board, I decided to approach the Nurse Managers in each district as being the professionals from the Health Board most likely to be able to contribute to the Review. They and their staff are closely involved with the community and the young children likely to require daycare services. They would know what type of provision mothers were looking for. In the course of their duties, they also co-operated closely with local GPs and would be aware of any issues arising from that section of the community.

Again, the response to my request was very mixed. There was no response from two areas but some others had obviously given the matter careful consideration and replied accordingly. I got the impression they were not sure as to the purpose of the Review, why they had been involved and how they could contribute.

Consultation also took place with local enterprise companies who are normally very supportive of services to parents returning to work. Most of the companies expressed a keen interest in the Review and were happy to help in any way they could. No response was received from two however, and this rather surprised me as one in particular had made a substantial financial contribution towards training in child care.

Trade unions exist to represent their members' views and interests and so I decided to contact nine of the best known unions in the region to elicit their views on the subject. I was extremely disappointed. Only 2 provided pertinent responses. Of these replies, one in particular, was very worthwhile and had obviously been given consideration as a matter of importance in relation to the work situation. However, the others displayed a lack of interest and understanding as to how this affected them.

On completing the consultation, we made every effort to incorporate the views of everyone who had taken the time and effort to contribute to this Review.

Committee Involvement

Following the Director of Social Work's report to the Social Work Committee on 30 April 1992, the Joint Sub-Committee on Pre-school Provision which is made up of Regional Council members from both Social Work and Education Committees, was considered to be the appropriate forum to discuss detailed issues arising from the Children Act 1989. At their subsequent meeting on 12 May 1992, members on the Sub-Committee discussed the implications of the Children Act with particular reference to their obligations under Section 19 of the Act. They were invited to consider (a) the proposal that their remit be extended to cover the needs of children under eight and (b) their involvement in the Review of childminding, daycare and education services for children under eight.

They agreed to recommend that their remit be extended to cover all children under eight and that the Highland Scottish Pre-school Play Association be invited to appoint an observer to the Sub-Committee for the purposes of the Review. In relation to the Review itself, they confirmed that only matters of principle concerning the Review would be submitted to the Sub-Committee.

The Joint Sub-Committee was not contacted again until the process was well underway and the Review actually taking shape. An outline report was then drawn up and presented to the Joint Sub-Committee on 24 November 1992 for their consideration and approval. The report included details of how the Review was being conducted in the Region and those involved in the preparation of the Review Report. The content was discussed and approval was given to continue with the report as proposed in the outline.

Once the consultation process was over, the questionnaires had been returned and all the information collated in the final draft report, we returned to the Joint Sub-Committee on 20 January 1993 with our report for their approval. Several members raised questions in relation to their respective areas. Possibly the report had focused attention on particular aspects of these services which perhaps had not been under such close scrutiny in the past. The Committee acknowledged there were deficiencies in the services and while appreciating the need for improving the provision, the financial implications prevented them from proceeding with any further development of ideas and plans. There were also several comments on the necessity for this Review and report.

Some minor alterations and corrections were necessary but, this apart, the Committee was quite satisfied with the final report and proposed it should be put forward to the parent committees for approval.

The amended report went before the Education and Social Work Committees respectively on 3 and 4 February, was accepted and passed to the full Council for final approval. Approval was granted.

Future Implications

Policy development and corporate planning

The duty to Review will ensure that daycare services for children under eight will come to the attention of the public and elected members no less frequently than three yearly.

The factual information which has been widely available through the Report is generally being used in identifying and acknowledging areas of need. There would seem to be signs that the independent and voluntary sectors, encouraged by the Local Enterprise Companies, are already making available services or are at the planning stage of provision to meet some of these needs. This is against the background of public debate on daycare provision which was not principally generated by the Section 19 Review.

Other than the Joint Sub-Committee extending their remit from pre-school provision to cover provision for the under eights, policy development within the Regional Council has not been altered in any way as a result of the duty to review. At this stage there would not appear to be any plans to do so, but there is a greater working together to be seen in respect of the Education, Social Work and Health Departments.

Quality and distribution

In the future, services should perhaps be able to move on from examining the quantity and location of provision to concentrating on the quality of the work being undertaken. This could be achieved by consultation with parents and children and by virtue of the inspections carried out in pursuance of Part X of the Children Act.

The application of Part X and Section 19 of the Children Act to Scotland in the absence of the general framework provided in England and Wales by the philosophy and full provision of the Act, has had only a limited effect on overall attitudes to children in Scotland. The thinking which lies behind the 1989 Act requires to be incorporated in full within Scotland so that daycare resources can be seen in an overall context of child care provision.

There is an increased confidence in the voluntary and independent sector with a recognition that they are the main providers of service and are registered as being competent in this field of work. This has been assisted by the increased availability of training in the field of child care and consequently an improvement in their public image and worth which has led to a greater self confidence in the individual carers.

Inter-agency working

As already mentioned, there has been a noticeable improvement in the inter-agency working between the statutory agencies but I would suggest this is also true of co-operation between statutory and voluntary agencies and also voluntary agencies with one another.

Many organisations have made contact with the Social Work Department advising of plans for service development, seeing Social Work, not as a provider of either the service or funds to develop the service, but, rather, as a catalyst to progressing their schemes.

In several instances the public meetings can take the credit for bringing organisations together to the benefit of daycare provision. There is no doubt that new links have been forged and inter-agency working has improved in terms of this service provision and much of it as a direct result of the Review. I would very much hope this pattern would continue.

A Learning Experience

Looking back over the experience now, I think there are several lessons to be learned.

Consultation was a major problem and securing opinions and contributions from the consumers of services proved to be almost impossible. It had been difficult enough eliciting responses from some of the professionals in the child care related fields so how could we expect spontaneous involvement in the review process from the ordinary public?

Perhaps we could go part of the way to solving this problem if we were to improve our publicity campaign because dissatisfaction relating to publicity of the Review was by far the most common reason for complaint. It would seem the publicity did not provide an adequate explanation about the Review nor did it reach a wide enough audience. A large percentage of the population knew nothing about the Review and many of these people did have children in the relevant age group. Dissemination of information about the Review must be a priority before the next Review. It should be distributed much earlier on in the process and should give clear indications as to the kind of information we hope to obtain and instructions about relaying the same to the co-ordinator of the Review.

The public meetings, although giving opportunity for discussion on daycare provision were quite restrictive and discriminatory in their execution for various reasons and the time was not available to increase the number of public meetings. The geography of the region is particularly difficult and therefore made it impossible for some people to attend the meetings due to distances involved. No account was taken of the difficulties shift workers may encounter in trying to attend. Single parents might also have found it a problem if there was nobody readily available to watch their children for the duration of the meeting. Whilst giving careful consideration to the promotion of quality daycare we should be arranging to make provisions for creche facilities at any future public meetings.

The guidelines produced by The Scottish Office were very helpful but in some respects were open to a variety of interpretations and provided too wide a base on which we had to work. There is a need for some form of standarisation of the Review format throughout Scotland in order to ensure the reports have some meaning in relation to one another and are of greater value to the general public in painting the overall picture of provision throughout the country.

Throughout the consultation period I was asked many times about the purposes of the Review and, being in the position of having to supply a response, I had cause to give the question much thought. The more I considered it, the more I realised that I too was not sure of the true purpose behind this statutory responsibility to review. Was it purely an information gathering exercise and once completed the reports would sit on a shelf somewhere gathering dust? Were the reports destined for sociological research? Was it a method of central government surveying and monitoring these services with a view to future planning? What of the funding implications? Would there be additional funding available to develop services as a result of the findings? I did suspect there might be elements of all these. There was also an expectation from several interested parties that this document would be a comprehensive directory of services and disappointment or even dissatisfaction was expressed when this turned out not to be the case.

On reflection, I tried to accomplish far too much in the short time available. The first year since the implementation of the Act was almost over and there was a feeling of urgency around to get the Review underway, the report completed and through the committee system before the end of March. Too much new ground had to be covered and new contacts made in the brief period available. Should I be the person to repeat the process for the 1995 Review, I would start the whole procedure much earlier and would allow plenty of time to carry out a more comprehensive consultation and research process. Ideally the review process should be ongoing between reports and provision for staff and the additional financial support to do this should be made by the government departments involved.

LOTHIAN REGION
Gary Pinnons, Principal Officer (Children and Families), Planning and Co-ordination Division

Introduction
In Lothian, work on the Review was carried out between February and October 1992 with the first report being published in May 1993. In the Education Department, the lead role was taken by staff from the primary and nursery division, with some assistance from community education. In the Social Work Department, the lead role was taken by the Planning and Coordination (Children) Section. No additional posts were created specifically for the Review, although the Social Work Department did commit additional hours between May and October, 1992.

Joint Working Arrangements
Lothian had from 1981 well established joint working arrangements between Education and Social Work, from the local "grass roots" level through to elected members. At local level, a network of mini Committees for the Under Fives (CFUF's) existed with representation from Education, Health, Social Work and the voluntary sector, and were chaired by senior officers from Education and Social Work. They reported to the Regional Joint Management Group for the Under Fives which had representation at senior level from Education, Health, Social Work and the Women's Unit. The Joint Management Group reported to the Joint Sub-Committee for Education and Social Work and Women's Committee on services for the under fives. A Joint Officer/Member Group had also been established to work on specific issues relating to services for the under fives.

This structure had been designed to improve co-ordination between Education and Social Work in matters concerning the under fives, and to facilitate links with health, voluntary bodies and other interested parties. It proved to be valuable during the review process, particularly in the data collection and consultation phases. However, in the initial planning for the first Review an obvious problem emerged. The structure had been designed to improve co-ordination in matters concerning the under fives, whereas Section 19 of The Children Act, 1989 required a Review of services for the under eights. Furthermore, the time scale set for the completion of the first Review was very tight. Lothian's response was to ask the existing Joint Officer/Member Group to oversee the review process, and to include in this Group representatives from organisations involved with five to eight year olds. This facilitated the establishment of working links between a number of the key organisations working in the under eights field, such as, organisations representing childminders, out of school providers, play schemes and play groups as well as representatives from Education, Social Work and elected members.

Policy Aims and Objectives

The Guidance from The Scottish Office required that the Review should be set within the context of agreed policy aims and objectives for services for the under eights. The Joint Officer/Members Group's first task was to revise Lothian's Policy Aims and Objectives Statement on the Under Fives to take account of issues relating to five- to eight-year-olds. The following policy goal and service provision objectives emerged:

1. The Regional Council is committed to working towards an integrated and universal service for under fives and their families which will have the flexibility to meet a variety of needs such as family support, provision for working parents and part-time pre-school experience. The Council is also committed to the promotion of quality out of school care provision for primary school age children.
2. All-daycare and related provision must offer a high standard of care and an appropriate learning environment.
3. All provision must be within an equal opportunities framework. Opportunities to address multi-cultural, anti-racist education should be promoted. Encouragement must be given to families from minority ethnic communities to use available services. In addition, the aim is to provide for children with special needs in main stream provision, subject to parental wishes.
4. There should be a range of accessible, affordable, flexible provision which takes into account the needs of parents who are working or studying.
5. Parents and carers should be actively involved in the planning and running of provision.
6. Accurate and up-to-date information must be readily available to parents and carers.
7. The local authority will work in partnership with central government, the Health Board, the voluntary sector, employers, private sector, service users and potential users to provide the range of services that are necessary.
8. Making available a place in an appropriate daycare setting for every child whose parents want it, is our ultimate objective. Day care is defined in Section 79(B) of the Children Act, 1989 as any form of care or activity supervised by a responsible person provided for children during the day, whether or not it is provided on a regular basis.

It was agreed that these policy aims and objectives would determine the future direction of work with the under eights in Lothian Region.

Data Collection

The data used for the first Review was not as comprehensive as we would have hoped, the main reason for this being the tight time scale set for completion of the first Review. The data presented in the report reflected the situation in Lothian as of 10 July 1992. To have allowed more time for data collection would have caused problems in completing the consultation process by October 1992.

It was relatively easy to gather data on Education Department provision (nursery schools and classes) and Social Work Department provision (children's centres and day carers). We were also able to get reasonably accurate data from the Community Care Registration and Inspection Service on provision that had to register under the previous legislation – childminders, independent nurseries and playgroups.

Data on 'out of school care' provision was made available from the All Lothian Out of School Care Association and Community Education but was not as comprehensive as we would have liked. Lothian Play Forum and Community Education provided reasonably complete information on play schemes. The majority of play schemes and out of school care clubs require, as a consequence of the Children Act, to be registered, but in July 1992 the Community Care Registration and Inspection Service had not started on this process, having concentrated on re-registering provision registered under the previous legislation. However, by the next Review report we expect that the Community Care Registration and Inspection Service will be able to provide comprehensive and accurate information on this provision.

Detailed and accurate information on creches was just not available in Lothian, but, as many will require to inform or register with the Community Care Registration and Inspection Service under the provisions of Part 10 of The Children Act, 1989, it is expected that, by the next Review, we will have access to good quality information on this provision.

We recognised that there is a wide range of other services which make a valuable contribution towards meeting the needs of the under eights. However, the time scales did not allow us to make a start on collecting and collating this type of information. Consideration will be given as to how to do this for future reviews.

The Guidance issued by The Scottish Office also required that attention be given to the daycare needs of children with special needs and for minority ethnic groups. However, few providers collected detailed information on children with special needs or children from minority ethnic groups, and it was therefore difficult to draw any firm conclusions on their usage of daycare provision. A consequence of this is that it is difficult to accurately monitor the effectiveness of the Region's policy on integration and equal opportunities. A Joint Education/Social Work Task Group is to be established to examine the issues of the information base for under eights provision and the issues relating to children with special needs and children from minority ethnic groups will be addressed as part of this process.

The data collection process also highlighted the need for establishing an agreed protocol for data collection to facilitate a more accurate measurement of the level of provision. This will require, for example, trying to reach agreement on a definition of terms like 'session', 'capacity', etc. A national working group has been established to do work on this issue and Lothian is contributing to this process.

Consultation

The consultation with interested organisations and individuals took place in two phases. The first was between February and July 1992 with the consultation being carried out in a variety of ways, including meetings, written requests, and radio broadcasts. General comments were sought on the existing provision for under eights and their families and were summarised in a chapter of the draft report. The second phase was during October 1992, when the draft report was circulated for further consultation. This process was successful, with a wide variety of organisations offering comment.

However, we were disappointed at the poor response from consumers and are committed to looking at methods of improving this for the next Review. Methods such as questionnaires and public meetings, rejected this time because of the limitations imposed by the time scale, will be used. Thought will also be given as to how we can achieve consultation with consumers about provision on an ongoing basis rather than seeking it every three years as part of the review process.

We were fortunate this time that the Low Pay Unit had completed a major survey on the child care requirements of working parents in late 1990 early 1991, and that Lothian was one of the regions which contributed. This survey provided valuable additional information for the consultation section of the Review report.

The issue raised most often by respondents was the dearth of good quality, low cost child care, particularly for the under threes and the five- to eight-year-olds. Comment was also received on issues relating to the level and spread of statutory provision; lack of awareness of the needs of children from minority ethnic groups; limitations on choice for children with disabilities; lack of good quality and accessible information on services; lack of training opportunities; concern about the standard of some provision; lack of emergency provision particularly for women and children leaving home because of violence; the particular problems of child care in rural areas.

Initial Analysis

The initial analysis of the demographic data, the data on provision and the information from the consultation process suggests a need for more low cost, good quality daycare, particularly for the under threes and the six- to seven-year-olds.

The demographic data projected an increase in the number of under eights between 1992 and 1995 with this increase particularly marked in relation to 0–3 year olds and 6–7-year-olds. The key role of daycare provision in an anti-poverty strategy was also identified, with figures showing some 30,906 children under 11 dependent on families eligible for income support. Of the 30,906, 18,922 are part of a one-parent household. An analysis of the data on the existing range of daycare provision suggested that Lothian Region is not equipped to meet the needs of those on low incomes, including those who are seeking to return to work as a way out of the poverty trap. Social Work Department provision, being part of a specific family support strategy, had precise admission criteria, while Education Department nursery provision had relatively few full-time places and with few exceptions only operated during the term time. The costs are high in the independent/private sector and voluntary provision such as play groups and parent and toddler groups are not structured to meet the requirements of parents seeking, or in, employment. After-school care provision was relatively under-developed and play schemes only operate during the holidays.

Lothian Region was aware of many of these issues prior to the Review and is committed to increasing nursery provision, further developing out of school provision and targeting community funded provision for the under threes. The findings from the first Review confirmed these as priority developments.

Lessons from the First Review

While acknowledging that neither the time, nor the expertise, was available to cover all that The Scottish Office Guidance required for the first Review, the Education and Social Work Departments welcomed the legal framework established, with its requirement to continuously review and monitor the provision; compare supply and demand and set realistic and achievable targets for service provision; work in partnership with other agencies; and consult with service users and others.

The first Review did meet the objective of raising the profile and awareness of issues relating to daycare provision for the under eights and the process demonstrated the value of existing joint working arrangements in Lothian. In many ways the process consolidated and strengthened these arrangements and facilitated the forming of new ones.

The process of reviewing highlighted a number of issues that required addressing to ensure that the next Review is more comprehensive. The key tasks here are:

1. Information: A comprehensive, commonly agreed database needs to be established. This data needs to be accessible to policy makers, planners,

service providers and consumers. A Joint Education/Social Work Task Group has been established in Lothian to take this forward.

2. Co-ordination: A Review is necessary of the membership and remit of the existing mini Committees for the Under Fives and the Divisional Coordinating Groups for the Under Fives, examining issues such as the involvement of consumers, representation from minority ethnic groups, and the establishment of effective local links with organisations representing five- to eight-year-olds. A Joint Education/Social Work Task Group has been established to undertake this Review.

3. Consultation: Thought needs to be given as to how consultation is arranged, and particularly how the views of service users are heard. Ideally, structures which allow for consultation on an ongoing basis are preferable to the seeking of views every three years.

The priorities for service development indicated by the first Review are:

1. Low cost, good quality daycare.
2. Provision for the threes and under.
3. An increase in out of school care provision.

As noted in this paper Lothian is committed to developing provision in these areas and it is hoped that there will be some measurable growth within the next Review period.

BORDERS REGION
Dr Sue Ross, *Assistant Director (Operations)*
Jimmy Hawthorn, *Principal Officer (Childcare)*

In writing about the impact of the Children Act requirements in Borders Region, we are not impartial assessors. We write this as managers charged with the responsibility of implementing new legislation in the light of Council policy and Departmental priorities, not independent observers of the process and outcomes we are describing. It is described here from the "inside" looking outwards by two players in a complex "game", which involved many players and which continues beyond the events and actions described here. We are not, in Gregory Bateson's (1970) famous phrase, "outside the ecology" for which we were planning. We will describe the process of implementation and the lessons and conclusions we have drawn from our experiences as we see it at this stage of the process. Some of what we describe here will echo themes from our fellow contributors to this book. Some of what we write will be specific to our Region, with its particular rural context. Some of what we conclude will have significance for managers and practitioners when they try to successfully operationalise legislative requirements to improve service delivery. The latter aim is our major objective in writing up this experience of under eights development in the Borders in the last three years. We hope that what we describe is not merely anecdotal for the reader and that it does give pointers as to how a service as complex as under eights can be influenced and changed by decision-making in the local government and central government context.

Our contribution falls into three sections. The first section describes the context and process of implementation of the Act. The second section gives our analysis of the point we believe we have reached in the development of under eights services at this time. The third section summarises some of the general themes and difficulties which we believe have been demonstrated by this process of trying to bring about these changes and improvements in services for under eights.

Description of the Process

Although the Children Act came into force in Scotland in October 1991, any attempt to understand the impact in the Borders must begin some years before. Borders Regional Council first established a working party for pre-school provision in 1987. This Working Party had representatives from both the Education and Social Work Departments, as well as Borders Health Board and the Borders Association of Pre-school Playgroups (as it was then called). The Working Party focused on three main issues:

- what was described as a "justification" for pre-school education;
- an analysis of the existing pattern of provision in Borders Region;
- a plan for improvements in services for pre-school children and their families.

The Working Party produced a report in April 1987, which was reported on to both Social Work and Education Committees and which established a Pre-school Advisory Group known as the Working Party for Under-Fives (WORPUF).

Both the Education and Social Work Committees accepted the recommendations of the 1987 report in principle. These were:

1. to adopt a policy of phased development on nursery education from 420 part-time places to 500
2. to accept greater financial responsibility for Borders playgroups
3. to assist voluntary organisations providing pre-school education
4. to facilitate discussion among groups involved with pre-school education in a variety of ways
5. to create a pre-school officer post within the Region

Between 1987 and 1991, some of the aims of the working group were achieved. Two out of the proposed four nursery classes were established and the Pre-school Playgroups Association were given increased financial support, enabling, by 1991, 26 playgroups to meet in accommodation available within primary schools throughout the Region. The Childminding Association representative was brought into the working group. Nine co-ordinating committees for under-fives were established, spread throughout the Region, giving a wider focus to the development of under-fives work in the voluntary sector.

The fifth objective of the creation of a pre-fives Development Officer was pursued by way of a submission to The Scottish Office for Section 10 funding, in collaboration with Children in Scotland (formerly the Scottish Child and Family Alliance). This approach to the creation of a post was based on a clear perception of the members of the Working party that mainstream funding from any of the statutory agencies (Social Work, Education or Health) would be unlikely to be successful. Included in the submission to The Scottish Office by Children in Scotland was an undertaking that a Link Group, made up of interested individuals, should be formed as a support group for the pre-fives Development Officer. It was also understood that a Voluntary Sector Forum, consisting of members drawn from a variety of voluntary organisations, with an interest in pre-school provision and other child care provision, would be established in the Borders.

By October 1990, when The Scottish Office informed local authorities of their obligations under the Children Act, it might be thought that Borders Region had a reasonable inter-agency structure from which to co-ordinate under-fives work. The Working Party had formally taken on a role of "adopting a corporate approach to the development of services for pre-school children", which also included a co-ordinating function for the activities of mainstream and voluntary pre-school provision, and the Children in Scotland Development Officer post was established.

The new legislative duties introduced by the Children Act should have been a spur for this work to flourish. In the event, however, the experience was rather less straight forward. (The process of implementation of the Act was unsatisfactory, despite the active work in the Borders to promote partnership in the development of under-fives services.) The first indications that the 1989 Children Act in England & Wales would have any significance in Scotland only came in 1990, when The Scottish Office promised a consultative document in June. In the event, the consultation came in November 1990, giving less than a year's implementation time. The effects of this were that the local authority had very little opportunity to consider its implications across the two main departments of Education and Social Work. In advance of the consultation being circulated, the Social Work Committee was asked, in October, to approve the creation of two new posts, to strengthen the registration and inspection duties and requirements from a social work perspective. These were approved by the Policy & Resources Committee in April 1991 and the people came into post in October 1991, just at the implementation point.

It must be stressed, however, that the creation of those two vital posts, which enabled the Social Work Department to achieve its statutory obligations under Part X of the Act, within the first year of implementation, were actually borne of a "guess" about the requirements of the Act. They sadly did not reflect joint initiative with Education to ensure the educative component of standard setting for playgroups, childminders and nurseries. Looking back, an opportunity was missed to create joint department resources between Social Work and Education, at the time of the new statutory duties being announced. Given the lack of consultation on the Act, neither Social Work nor Education staff considered a joint initiative. Given the lead-up time required for Regional Councils to define their requirements for new resources and to bring these new resources into being, the eleven-month consultation process was less than helpful and greatly contributed to opportunities being lost for the Council to consider its new obligations and duties.

Similarly, it was only in June 1991 that the Guidance on the Act was published. In terms of planning time scales and local government Committee cycles, this, effectively, meant that Committees would not be informed of their new duties until October, when they were scheduled for implementation. In October, the Social Work Committee gave permission for two further posts to deal with the pressures caused by the increased regulation of under-eights facilities. These were appointed in September 1992, almost a further year down the track of implementation.

The additional resources thus created were all about the increased regulatory requirements of Part X, in relation to approval and inspection of under-eights facilities. Since no new central government resources accompanied the Act, the local authority had to meet the major operational requirements of the additional responsibilities from its own financial resources. However, the duties involved in the creation and publication of the Review in October 1992 were not able to be met by any additional resources. This created a particular problem for Borders Social Work Department, whose very small planning and information resources were fully utilised with the requirements of community care planning and consultation. The consequence of this was that the Review of under-eights was a considerable additional operational burden, to be met within the child care resources of a small department.

Turning now to the Review of Services required under Section 19 of the Act, a factual description might indicate a well-structured approach to the process, which is in no way indicative of the near panic experienced by those responsible for writing the report! As a discrete piece of work, the Section 19 Review of Services was completed in March 1993, when a copy of the consultation document was forwarded to The Scottish Office. The Review itself was finished in October 1992, when it received the formal approval of the Social

Work and Education Committees. In retrospect, the completion of the Review to timetable was an impressive achievement in itself, and the collaboration involved, both planned and fortuitous, will be addressed later. A more detailed brief based on the Review outline in The Scottish Office Guidance was presented to the Education and Social Work Committee in January 1992.

In acknowledgement of the fact that the Act extended the regulatory functions from under-fives to under-eights, the Early Years Advisory Group (EYAG) was set up in December 1991, and the responsibility for oversight of the Review process was delegated to this group of officers and members. In line with The Scottish Office Guidance that elected members be closely involved in the process, the vice-chairpersons of both Committees were co-opted on to the Group. The officers had recommended this action as a means of ensuring that early years issues were firmly part of the local political agenda and with the intention of ensuring the involvement and commitment of the key elected members. This group therefore became the focus for steering the Review and reporting back in due course to the respective Committees.

In October 1992, as well as approving the draft Review report, the Committees agreed that the Report be available for widespread consultation over a two-month period, with a summary of comments received forwarded to The Scottish Office. The consultation included district councils; community councils; local voluntary groups; leafleting of parents through schools; whilst publicity was through the local radio and press.

Some minor biographical and organisation details might help place the earlier systematic account in a more interesting local context. The Adviser for Early Education and Principal Officer – Child Care were the key operational staff from Education and Social Work. The former had worked in the Region for some years and played an important role in the setting up of WORPUF. Responsibilities related to the Review for this officer were a bolt-on to many other responsibilities.

The Principal Officer – Child Care started in post four months prior to the Children Act. Within one month the Principal Officer was joined by a Principal Planning Officer and Information Officer. By October 1991 the Principal Officer had recruited the Region's first two community child care officers, and the real voyage of discovery that was to become the Section 19 Review had begun.

The quantitative material collected for the Review drew extensively from the *Family Matters* survey which was prepared for Borders Regional Council by Children in Scotland and published in December 1991. This was a survey of child care and employment and training within Borders Region and was targeted at families with pre-school children. Interestingly, although it revealed a high level of satisfaction with the quality of existing services, the majority of respondents wanted an increase both in the volume and range of existing services. The process of re-registration undertaken by the newly–appointed community child care officers reinforced the finding that the quality of daycare provision – childminding, playgroups and private day nurseries – was mostly of a satisfactory standard, and in many cases impressive. To date, the more vigorous regulatory overview has not led to a decrease in provision as might have been expected, and the general impression is that daycare providers have welcomed this increased involvement of Social Work staff in their day-to-day work with children.

The existence of a committed voluntary sector provision, albeit a fragmented one, provided invaluable source material both in terms of quantitative information on provision as well as more qualitative information on the range of daycare offered, and its variable nature. For example, some playgroups had initially permanent and exclusive access to premises such as spare school accommodation, enabling them to offer a far more comprehensive range of facilities than those which operated from temporary and cramped premises where all the equipment had to be packed away after each session. Moreover, some playgroups had use of the accommodation free, whereas rental charges for others necessitated an endless round of fund-raising to ensure equipment was replaced and suitable.

The most positive observation on the Review as a process would say that it represented a sharp learning curve for all those involved in its preparation. It resembled a church committee's attempts at organising a large summer fete, with Education and Social Work staff beavering away on the collection of data, ably assisted by representatives from the voluntary sector and the Children in Scotland Development Officer. Towards the end of this process, the Information Officer within the Social Work Department offered invaluable support in collating statistical information from the General Register Office, and presenting this in the form of maps and tables. The Educational input was provided by a staff member who had been seconded to Headquarters following the Departure of the Adviser for Early Education. As a seconded teacher, she was actually on holiday whilst the Review was being written up, but provided her department's information during the first weeks of her holiday. The Principal Officer – Child Care worked initially full-time for three weeks to draw the Review together into a coherent document, leaving the Assistant Director (Operations) to take over his other operational responsibilities.

In terms of what has been learned for the next Review, an officers' group led by Education and Social Work, and involving other key players, has been set up to plan the work for October 1995. The Principal Officer – Child Care will continue to have a key role in the planning, alongside other operational responsibilities, and Education similarly will allocate this work to a recently-appointed Adviser for whom the Review work will continue to be a bolt-on.

Where are we Now? An Evaluation of the Process

The introduction of new legislation requirements for under-eights services ought to have significantly assisted the development of higher quality services within an authority like Borders, where aspiration to develop and improve resources was already clearly established. In one way it can be shown that this has been the case in respect of the requirements for the regulation and inspection of the under-eights market and the raising of standards for those involved in delivery of services, childminders, playgroup leaders, nursery and family centre staff.

The other major implication of the Act, however, was to require local authorities to create and maintain a co-ordinated structure for under-eights work across agencies. To this end, the duty to review services should have had a major role in ensuring that an infrastructure for this was established. For a variety of reasons, this has not been successful to date. Some of the reasons for this are discussed below.

The review requirement occurred within a policy vacuum in the Scottish context. The Children Act, from which it sprang, was not part of the Scottish legislative requirements for child care. Similarly, the responsibility for the provision of pre-school facilities is still largely viewed as a private matter for individual parents throughout most of Scotland. Whilst good public provision does exist in pockets, where it has been developed, largely through the voluntary sector, or through particular political initiatives such as the PICC project in Fife, the national picture is patchy and piecemeal. The view in the Borders would appear to support the notion that pre-school child care remains the responsibility of parents, except where they are unfit to undertake that responsibility as, for example, in the case of children on the "at risk" register, who are given access to subsidised resources and to some limited family centre provision. This policy position and lack of an alternative, positive view of under-eights service is a significant limiting factor to developing co-ordination of purpose and services for under-eights, despite the commitment that we as officers must express given its central importance to underpin good child care provision.

Similarly, the dislocation of any planning structures for children, particularly across the sectors of Health, Social Work and Education, have tended to categorise and limit services within the greatest responsibilities of those agencies. They have required development of ad hoc responses like those described above. Young children with special needs and their families, for example, tend to fall between the provision of health care and social care, rather than receiving complementary or joint-funded resources for, say, respite services. In particular, local authority committee structures, which keep Social Work and Education matters separate, mean joint approaches are difficult.

In Borders, several of the reports to Committee over the last three years about under-eights matters have been jointly presented by the Directors of Education and Social Work. This, in part, addresses the structural problem, but it still means that children's needs are categorised through departmental concerns rather than in the rounder context of children's rights and needs within society and their local communities.

The diversity of interests in the under-eights field is another major difficulty in co-ordinating and developing resources. The first Review of Services in Borders demonstrated the diversity of provision across the voluntary, private and statutory services. Creating co-ordinating groups which are representative of these diverse interests is fraught with difficulties. For example, the playgroup movement in Borders region is an area of voluntary activity which enjoys the support of the elected members, despite the lack of a broader political agenda in relation to child care services for under-eights. It is particularly important, therefore, that in assisting a voluntary organisation to develop and contribute to the planning process, that other important groups, whose interests are less well represented, are not disenfranchised from playing a similarly important role. In Borders, the development of training as a precursor for SVQs has attracted representation from playgroups, childminders, the private nurseries and local authority family centres. This mix of interests must be maintained, though this at times is difficult to achieve, bearing in mind that they are all competing for scarce resources.

What can be Learnt from this Process of Change?

The critical points we would highlight from the process described above are as follows:

1. The imposition of a range of new statutory duties by Central Government on local government services, without additional resources and with no satisfactory lead-in time, creates significant additional pressures which usually means the standard of other work falls and vital decisions about resources are rushed.

2. The impact of new statutory duties can open up increased difficulties along "fault-lines" which already exist. In this case in Borders, these fault-lines are the significant problems created by the limited local political mandate to resource under eights initiatives within the Regional Council.

3. The requirement to "review" services, but not to provide standards or measures against which that review could be carried out, means that the exercise becomes inevitably descriptive, rather than part of the development of a co-ordinated strategic planning framework.

4. The responsibility for the implementation of the Children Act has almost entirely fallen to Social Work Department. Despite good working relationships

in Borders with Education colleagues and significant levels of good-will and commitment, the Act does not locate responsibility for the broad educative requirements of child care clearly within the Education Department's remit. This marginalises its significance and will inevitably create inappropriate pressures on Social Work Departments to concentrate provision on socially disadvantaged children, rather than on all children. This brings the added problems of stigmatising family centre resources and local authority nurseries and child care centres.

5. The "tartanisation" of a small part of the Children Act in a piecemeal way in Scotland brings a legislative requirement which does not address the Scottish context and is not developed as part of a consistent approach to child care. The wider debate about the future of the White Paper on child care, *Scotland's Children,* must take on board under eights services as part of the overall context of child care provision.

6. Services which are planned and developed in a political vacuum at both national and local level are invariably fragmented and piecemeal. No amount of requirements to review and publish plans can produce consistency of purpose, when the need for those services has not been established and agreed. In Borders, the *Family Matters* survey clearly demonstrated the needs of parents of young children, for affordable, good quality child care, but the prioritisation of that need within the policy objectives of the service plans of the Council has not yet been established. This is greatly hindered by the lack of demonstrable commitment by Central Government to the basic child-care requirements of under eights in Scotland at this time.

7. There is a real danger of increasing regulatory mechanisms over services, without additional resources, to train and develop staff working in these services. In Borders we have been fortunate to date, in that we could offer new training initiatives with the assistance of the Education Department and the independent sector, for childminders, playgroup leaders and nursery staff. If, for any reason, this development falls away, or funding is unavailable, we could be in a position of limiting, through proper inspection and registration requirements, a shrinking market of providers. It is vital that this does not occur, or young children and their parents will lose out on the very limited choices available to them at present.

Conclusion

From the description we have given of the process of development of under-eights provision in Borders Region, it will be clear that many difficulties remain. The infrastructure to develop co-ordinated under eights services does not exist for many reasons. In the absence of a major injection of resources, driven by policy considerations, both of which are unlikely in the current climate, there would appear to be difficulties ahead in sustaining local efforts despite the Review duties and the public accountability which that brings. That said, the commitment to improve standards in partnership with the voluntary sector, in line with the wishes of parents and children, has been significantly developed since early efforts of the Working Party in 1987. It is our belief that the desire and need for higher quality affordable child care, which has been demonstrated to exist even in the rural communities in the Borders, will continue to find a greater voice within both the local and central government context. It remains our priority to ensure that we are able and ready to respond to any opportunities which might develop as a result of such demands.

Chapter 3

$\blacklozenge$

BEING INVOLVED IN THE PROCESS

All authorities were required to involve fully in the review process other agencies in the voluntary sector, the private sector and other interested local authority departments. This chapter looks at that involvement from the point of view of those who were participants.

Large voluntary organisations, e.g. the Scottish Pre-school Play Association and the Scottish Childminding Association, are well represented. However, the Health Boards make a smaller contribution, as do District Council Leisure and Recreation Departments, and Regional Council Planning Departments and Chief Executive Departments. There seems, to some degree, to be a general lack of appreciation that the Review is relevant in any serious way to the work of these bodies. Equally, there is not generally an understanding that services provided by these bodies for young children are best approached corporately, in a way that involves other agencies or local authority departments.

It is also the case that, in the process of forging new relationships across agencies and departments, for the process of carrying out the Review, it was less easy to do this where there was not already a tradition of working together. This was often the case when it involved Health Boards and, even more so, local authority departments other than Education and Social Work.

Nevertheless, the review process was the catalyst for a remarkable degree of inter-agency and inter departmental collaboration, which, in many instances, represented a new approach.

STRATHCLYDE REGION

Strathclyde Early Years Voluntary Sector Forum
Julie Collis

The Strathclyde Early Years Voluntary Sector Forum has 55 member organisations and employs a development officer, and was therefore ideally placed to assist in both the review process and the consultations on the draft document. It was closely involved in all aspects of the Children Act and fully consulted throughout the review process, and nominated representatives to serve on multidisciplinary working groups. Progress reports were presented to the Forum by education officers. Forum members were fully informed by our regular newsletters and opportunities were given for comment.

The Forum assisted by producing the section in the Review on training in the voluntary sector and by consulting with members. The Forum organised a major seminar as part of the consultative process which was attended by 46 participants. The seminar concentrated on the section of the report *The Way Forward* as this raised many important issues for the voluntary sector since it is unlikely that the local authority will have the resources to expand services of their own. Main comments from Forum members and the discussion groups emphasised the following points:

- The Review did not contain enough information on provision for children with special educational needs.
- Work is still needed to achieve effective partnership between the voluntary sector and the region.
- The public image and understanding of childcare needs to be improved.
- The Review did not contain sufficient information on the contribution to services made by the voluntary sector.

Responses from individual Forum members were collated into a Forum response, taking into account the results of the seminar and both written and verbal comments from members. A more comprehensive list of voluntary sector organisations was compiled by the Forum and included a brief description of each organisation. Sections on *Training in the Voluntary Sector* and the overview of the work of the voluntary sector were re-written by the Forum Development Officer. The section on *The Way Forward* now takes account of the findings of the seminar and the proposed reorganisation of local government.

Looking back, the Review was conducted in an atmosphere of partnership and co-operation. It had to be accepted that this was the first Review and was being carried out to very tight timescales. Hopefully, the voluntary sector will have more time to comment and contribute next time round. Certainly, the existence of a structure such as the Forum makes the consultation exercise more effective.

Inevitably the Review showed gaps in provision, both in rural and inner city areas. It is difficult to see how the regional council will be able to increase provision in the current economic climate. The partnership with the voluntary sector will need to develop further if provision is to be expanded. The Review did not address the issue of quality this time. However, with the inspection procedures now in place, the information should be available for the next Review in three years' time. This will coincide with the reorganisation of local government. The suggestion made at the joint seminar that a working group of the Forum be set up to monitor progress could be one way to ensure a continuity and consistency of approach even through the upheaval reorganisation will inevitably bring.

Strathclyde SPPA
Eileen McKenna

The involvement of the Voluntary Sector in the working groups set up by Strathclyde Regional Council towards implementing the Children Act has been very valuable both to the Regional Council and ourselves. Continuous discussion of the effects of implementation on organisations providing for children 0–8 years helped towards a shared understanding of the more contentious issues and the formation of the most acceptable way to proceed within the dictates of the Act.

I was involved in discussions outwith Strathclyde and therefore had some access to the type of involvement taking place in other regions. This certainly underlined the value of having a distinct Pre-five Services Unit and an established Voluntary Sector Forum. This structure allowed an easier and more valuable interchange. SPPA was involved in the Member/Officer Group which preceded the Pre-Five Unit and has had a representative on the Pre-five Sub-Committee since its inception. This is a recognition of the complementary service we provide and the liaison we have with the Regional Council reflects this.

Each Division of our organisation was approached and responded individually to the consultation document. Their comments were primarily directed to the correction and addition of the listed services in their area. The Pre-Fives Services were generous and helpful in their allocation of copies of the regional and divisional documents. Each Regional Council Division had some form of consultation with the voluntary sector. Ayr Division held a large seminar for all interested parties in their area. I was invited to be one of the speakers at this.

SPPA were also represented in the Strathclyde Early Years Voluntary Sector Forum consultation. The requirement of the Review and the consultation exercise, whilst increasing the workload of the local authority and voluntary personnel, proved to be of major value in recording the childcare services in Strathclyde which will provide a basis for the future development of these services.

SPPA welcomes the recognition of the need for providers to work in partnership. We also agree with the need to form new partnerships. We would, therefore, wish to be involved in any discussions pertaining to future partnerships in the provision of local childcare services.

We welcome the recognition in the Review of the effects of The Children Act on voluntary organisations. We are willing to be a full partner in the implementation of the Act but we are seriously concerned as to how we will be able to meet the demands of the legislation in terms of increased direct support and input to our groups and increased training needs. We, therefore, hope that consideration is given to these extra demands when determining the level of future voluntary sector grants.

Scottish Childminding Association, Strathclyde
Marjorie Gregg

The Review appears to pay particular dividends in relation to the registration and inspection process where there were real worries that good childminders were being lost to the system. When new registration and inspection procedures were brought in concerns were raised as to how childminders would react to the changes and what was going to happen if any of them had real problems. We lost some very good childminders due to misunderstandings about what was required. However, the Review process has brought closer links between our organisation and the Pre-Fives Unit and other Under-Eights organisations. We now work hand in hand, any changes or problems are discussed fully. Shortcomings in communication between agencies have now been overcome.

Not withstanding the closer links, there are still grievances felt by childminders concerning some of the requirements for registration. They say that they are registering the childminders and not the premises yet they ask us to make changes that some of us feel are not necessary. Future reviews should take account of the need for appropriate and consistent information for childminders. There is a need to make sure that all concerned have all the relevant information required and that everyone receives the same information.

Lanarkshire Health Board
Helen Scott

The extent to which other organisations and agencies were involved in compiling the Review necessarily varied dependent on the amount of relevant information held by them. The extent to which the Health Board was involved varied from one area to another with statistical information being sought in one and service provision only in another. Involvement was not wholly satisfactory with discrepancies in the types of information elicited from the Board not fully explained.

The experience highlighted the need for both local and area communication of a much higher degree than at present. Locally this issue is being addressed and a joint collaborative working approach is emerging. At area level there still appears to be the need to develop a better communications network.

The Review highlighted that the quality and distribution of services is at present unequal. Collaborative inter-agency working should redress this balance.

The effect of the duty to review must positively improve the quality of inter-agency collaboration and joint working. The lesson to be learned is that on going communication and consultation between all agencies is absolutely vital in providing such a critical document which has to be used for future planning.

Glasgow Parks and Recreation, Glasgow City Council
Ian Hooper

Initially the main concern felt by those involved with registration of activities under the Children Act 1989 was regarding the seemingly ambiguous nature of the relevant areas of the Act. The Parks and Recreation Department, Glasgow City Council, offers a wide variety of activities for children of all ages within its facilities. It was quickly established through meetings with Strathclyde Regional Council, Department of Education, Pre-Fives Services that coached/taught activities held within Sports/Recreation Centres and swimming pools would not require to register. After several meetings and exchanges of correspondence with representatives from the Pre-Fives Services it was eventually decided that activities operated by the Parks and Recreation Department within recreation centres were not required to register at present because of their casual nature, whereas the majority of children's activities operated by external organisations would require to register. This had several implications for the Department, primarily that of building inspection. The Pre-Fives Service also recommended that the Council adhere to guidelines for supervision levels, number of children in centres, regardless of the nature of activities operated. One of the main problems was the huge scope of the Act and the fact that it is open to very different interpretations by the various registering authorities. Another difficulty is the lack of more specific information on the various applications of the Children Act, which may be due to the fact that the scope of the entire Act was wider for England than for Scotland. However, difficulties aside, the Children Act Review proved a useful exercise in terms of identifying existing provision and providing a more uniform/corporate approach to provision for under eights.

TAYSIDE REGION

SPPA, Tayside
Catherine Murray

Tayside SPPA reps had a meeting quite early on with the two Development Officers, one from Social Work and one from Education, who were appointed to produce the Review document. The meeting served to let us find out that their main role was to produce the Review Document, and set up the framework for inter-agency working, in the form of a Regional Under-Eights Working Group, with three under-eights District Fora feeding into it. It also served to let us all get to know each other, and helped future contact between us.

I gave them information about the history of playgroups and SPPA, about the positive and negative sides of playgroups, and about what needs to be different. I also supplied them with statistics about our member groups in Tayside.

Our fieldworkers were asked to make phone contact with their playgroups to get 'snapshot' attendance figures one week in June 1992, but this came with very short notice at a very busy time for fieldworkers and playgroups, and they had to say no. Instead they offered to post questionnaires to their playleaders. This offer was turned down for the questionnaire, but accepted for a letter sent out explaining about the Review, and preparing the playleaders to receive a questionnaire in September, as well as giving them advance notice that consultation meetings would be organised later in the year to discuss the Review findings. The Development Officers were invited to attend a Fieldworker In-Service Day later in June, to discuss the best way to get playgroup figures.

There were nine consultation meetings across the Region, and representatives of playgroups and SPPA attended these with other members of the public. At one of these meetings, we were given the chance to give a presentation about the value of playgroups and SPPA, and the problems we face.

The Under-Eights Working Group examined and discussed the Draft Review Document when it came out, and made some recommendations for inclusion in it. Being part of that group I was able to suggest that a paragraph about SPPA, as the support organisation for playgroups, would be a useful addition, and this was taken on board for the Final Review.

Sub-groups of the Regional Under-Eights Working Group were set up earlier this year to look at the five main issues which came out of the Review, and a good working relationship seems to have evolved from these. Work on establishing the District Fora has also begun. We receive a grant from Social Work to enable us to take part in co-ordination and liaison meetings regarding the Children Act, without dipping into our core funding which comes from Community Education.

Overall, I would say that the Children Act 1989 has brought our organisation into a much closer working relationship with the Departments of Social Work and Education, and other under-eights agencies. Apart from the Regional Under-Eights Working Group meetings, we have regular meetings with Social Work Quality Assurance Unit staff regarding registration and inspection issues, and we have links now with the Education Department through developing with them an induction course for playleaders. This course is recognised by the local authority as being a minimum requirement for playleaders, who do not have formal child care or education qualifications. We have always had close links with Community Education, and this year they obtained three yearly funding for us. This has been a great help in terms of future planning.

We feel that a pattern for consultation regarding future policy has now been established. Although we do not expect changes to happen overnight, it does appear to be a step in the right direction. It is also quite possible that services will develop, with this duty to review. The consultation process has highlighted some gaps in provision. The setting up of the District Fora is possibly going to help identify other gaps. Steering groups may be set up from these who will try and come up with innovative ideas in childcare, especially in rural areas.

The main problem, as always, will be one of resourcing, but it may be that District Fora and the Regional Under-Eights Working Sub-Groups will be able to feed back recommendations to the Regional Under-Eights Working Group regarding economical ways of filling some of the gaps. In turn, the Regional Under-Eights Group may make some recommendations to the policy makers regarding redistribution of existing resources in a way which could benefit more families.

As yet, this is all hypothetical, since the District Fora are still in their infancy, and they have the massive task of trying to talk to a good cross-section of parents to assess an overall picture of parental preference, while still keeping in mind the needs of the children.

Tayside SPPA has reaped benefits in terms of recognition and consultation, which have come through the local authority's duty to review daycare.

Tayside Health Board
M B Tannahill, Deputy Chief Area Nursing Officer

I would agree that reviewing policy and procedures in a multi-professional group can only lead to a better quality of service. In this particular area, group support is essential within a multi-professional group.

Joint education in child protection issues is a principle feature within Tayside. In addition, other areas in which we are working jointly with the local authority are: strengthening team work in child protection and methods of monitoring child protection plans once agreed.

HIGHLAND REGION

The description of the involvement of the Scottish Childminding Association in Highland Region was based on an interview between the Rural Tutor and the conductor of the Review, Carole Taylor.

Scottish Childminding Association, Highland Region,
Katie Adam

I was the only contributor for the section on Scottish Childminding Association as I was the only full-time member of staff in the Region. The contribution included brief details of the organisation and details of problems incurred during registration under the Children Act 1989. The details supplied were relevant to Highland Region only.

I was only able to attend one of the Review Consultation meetings. The meeting was held in Broadford, Isle of Skye, and I was working in that area at the same time. The content of the discussion was very stimulating and I introduced the idea of an Under Eights Forum for the Region. This was favourably commented on but I have not seen or heard any evidence of any progress so far.

The turnout to the meeting was very poor and I felt strongly that this was due to very little publicity and information to the public. I'm sure that if more publicity had been given, including information on the format/purpose of the Review, then a great number of interested parties would have made a more widespread contribution.

The statistics contained in the Review may be misleading due to the way in which information was gathered. For example only one childminder in Inverness had returned the questionnaire and it would seem from the published result that there were only three childminding places available. It may also have been beneficial to each organisation if there had been a contact address/telephone number given for each organisation e.g. in an index. Whereas statistics and basic information on services are beneficial and useful in some areas, the main aim of the Children Act and thence the Review was to address the quality of childcare services in each area.

Each agency mentioned in the Review document would seem to be very aware of the quality of their service; but is somewhat restricted in its aims by lack of funding. In that respect it would be a major step forward in quality childcare if the two departments were able to address the need for relevant and high quality training for staff and volunteers in the field.

I do not wish to be over critical of the report. I enjoyed an excellent working relationship with all the staff in the Social Work Children's Section and I would like to say that I have issued copies to many colleagues and childminders in the region. I am sure they will have found it a useful publication to refer to.

Highland Scottish Pre-school Play Association
Ann Brady

Within Highland Region, Highland Scottish Pre-school Play Association (HSPPA) supports and advises 210 pre-school groups catering for the needs of some 5,000 children under five. HSPPA's central office is housed within Highland Region's Social Work Children Services Department. This day-to-day contact between our voluntary organisation and the statutory services is a major contributing factor to the strong working relationship that exists between the two.

HSPPA was consulted and involved in discussions prior to the initial drafting of the Social Work Department's registration policy and guidelines. Our first contact regarding the review process came in June 1992 when representatives of HSPPA met with the Assistant Director of Children's Services to discuss ways HSPPA should be involved with the Review.

Between the end of June and mid August, our groups break for the summer holidays. It is also a time of great change with children leaving playgroup and entering full-time education, and new parents and children being introduced to the playgroup culture. We were therefore compelled to withhold group contact regarding the Review until after the beginning of the new session in mid-August. Forward planning would have allowed some contact before the end of the session in June and given more time to implement a thorough procedure.

A questionnaire was drafted, approved by the Social Work Department and sent out to our eight branches in August. (Branch Committees are made up of representatives from each group in their area.) Information was sought regarding numbers of children, premises, needs and priorities, waiting lists, etc. and collated by HSPPA to provide a profile of HSPPA's current childcare situation within Highland Region. This was then passed on to the Social Work Department. Confusion arose, however, when Councils of Voluntary Services were approached directly by Social Work and asked for information regarding childcare groups in their respective areas. As a result some of our groups were targeted a second time.

Public meetings were advertised throughout the Region by the Social Work Department. However, there was misunderstanding regarding the meeting agenda due to poor wording. The advertisements also gave limited notice and only by personally telephoning key representatives throughout the Region were HSPPA assured of attending all but one of these meetings. Disappointingly the turnout from the general public was poor.

There seemed to be a feeling of expectation from the public as to the Review producing positive action to improve childcare within their area. When the Review did not produce any immediate results, frustration crept in. More feedback is needed to keep people informed.

A clear communication system between the statutory agencies and all voluntary organisations providing childcare needs to be established. Forward planning is essential and adequate time needs to be set aside to ensure the problems experienced at this initial Review are not repeated.

HSPPA enjoys a sound working relationship with the Social Work Department. By building on that, hopefully some of the initial problems will not occur in the future.

BORDERS REGION

Borders Early Years Voluntary Sector Forum
Pat Newton

The Borders Early Years Voluntary Sector Forum was established as one of the strands of the Children in Scotland Pre-Fives Development Project, slightly ahead of the implementation of the Children Act, in Scotland. As was stated in the Borders Review document, the Forum should be able to offer a collective view for all voluntary organisations working with children.

It was asked to collate the views of all member groups, about the draft Review of Services document, and then make a corporate response. It was an almost impossible task. Timing was already out of phase, many of the members at that time had not been directly affected by the Children Act and therefore did not have any strong point of view, or were pressed for time and did not submit a response. An open discussion meeting was held to consider the draft but this was poorly attended. However, those views expressed were represented to the Social Work and Education Departments and included in the final documentation which went on to The Scottish Office.

I believe that the difficulties we had in gathering responses from the different voluntary bodies were associated with the problems of the stage of development of the Voluntary Sector Forum itself. Had our own structure been clearly mapped out, the influence would have been too strong to ignore. As things were, our collective voice was not giving clear messages.

The value of having in place a Voluntary Forum, representing the views of all childcare organisations, is not in question. When one reads documents from other areas, where a strong Forum makes a clear contribution to planning, there can be unquestionable benefits. It is to be hoped that by the next Review, the Forum will have wider representation and a definite place in the consultation process.

Undoubtedly, inter-agency working is a way forward. It has to be, however, that all partners are equal partners and that each one is clear about its role in the scheme of things. Those in the voluntary sector should be treated with respect and given appropriate status in the consultation process. It is not sufficient for the dialogue to be on peripheral issues as an afterthought! Inter-agency working can only prove to be influential and effective, once policies have been made and the structure for addressing issues is in place. When one can only raise issues and discuss them without changes being implemented, frustration and tensions follow.

Scottish Pre School Play Association, Borders
Pat Newton

The Review of Services document in Borders leaned heavily upon and drew extensively from the findings reported in the *Family Matters* survey, published in

December 1991, and on the work of the Pre-Fives Development Project. Whilst the survey was innovative and interesting, it sought only to explore the views of parents with small children.

SPPA's view was that the Review document relied too heavily on *Family Matters* and did not address the providers perspective in sufficient depth. As the support agency for the major providers of childcare in Borders (along with childminders), our contribution to the scenario, e.g. through the development of the Foundation Course for Carers and our own training programme, was not reported. The sole reference to SPPA was incorrect! There had been little or no consultation with the providers themselves, at the preparation phase of the Review. By the time the draft Review document appeared, the timing was already out of phase and there was no opportunity to discuss, only to submit written comment, though SPPA contributed to the open discussion meeting organised by the Voluntary Sector Forum.

The Children Act, with all the changes it encompassed for providers of childcare, was implemented with little information or consultation or investment of cash, where it mattered. This lack of real information and guidance produced tensions and fears. Parents, committees and playgroup leaders would have welcomed opportunities to share their experiences, worries and fears, with others in the same field, even though they lacked time and perhaps expertise and confidence to write comments. Perhaps some important aspects of the consultative process were omitted. There was minimal consultation with the "grass roots", in the voluntary organisations such as my own. The two major contributors to the reviewing process, Education and Social Work seemed largely to consult with each other.

The major shortcoming of the Review process concerns the raised expectations about the future of childcare caused by the Children Act and its trappings. The investment needed to implement the changes required has not been forthcoming. Borders Regional Council has not shown itself ready to act upon the recommendations of the review process to establish an infrastructure for childcare. In that respect, therefore, the Review has not moved things forward.

Borders Health Board

Dr Adrian Margerison

The key statement in the Border Review of Services concerns the creation of a strategic planning framework for developments in the statutory and independent sectors. The key to services for children in the pre-school and early schools groups will be what developments are deemed to be necessary, but in part any developments will be dependent on the other points that are made including both training initiatives and of course consideration of how to resource not only future reviews, but necessary developments in service, e.g. to develop nursery education for the 181 children currently on the waiting lists and the many more who are not only eligible but whose mothers see no point in applying as they know that they will not get a place.

I think that it is important that the Board maintains close links with the Borders Regional Councils Education and Social Work Departments in terms of development of services for children as Community Child Health is always dependent in part on the services available for children within the area of what might be broadly referred to as education and social work needs.

LOTHIAN REGION

Lothian Community Child Health

Dr Patricia D Jackson

We are fortunate in Lothian that the need for inter-agency work for matters relating to children has been recognised by Education, Health and Social Work for a number of years, and there is a system of locality teams involving the three agencies in discussions of issues relating to under-fives, which links into a central joint liaison committee for under fives. In view of the requirements of the Children Act it seemed logical to alter the remit of the joint liaison group to include issues relating to children under eight years of age. Although the Health Board is not a provider of daycare services to children to be reviewed under the terms of the act, the importance for the healthy development of children within their families is strongly influenced by the provision of good quality daycare and therefore the health service has a strong interest in the provision of these services. It was therefore encouraging to be involved in the initial review process and the subsequent setting up of a Forum to elucidate quality standards for the subsequent review of provisions in Lothian region.

In the initial review period the views of the Community Paediatric Department were sought in relation to the current daycare provisions and whether there were any gaps that we would identify in the type of services offered and our views on any required future development. Doctors and their nursing colleagues in the community were consulted. The time scale for the consultation was unfortunately rather short. This highlighted the difficulties in rapid communication from locality groups to central committees and necessitated many individual responses rather than a co-ordinated response on behalf of a particular group, and possibly further discussions. However, the final report, after consultation, seemed to well reflect the views that had been channelled back to the Social Work Department.

The process highlighted the following:

1. It was much easier to gain information about services to under fives rather than services for 5–8-year-olds outwith the school situation.

2. The structures for inter-agency work relating to under fives with special needs appeared to be quite well established. Recent development of the district based multidisciplinary teams for under fives with special needs had encouraged inter-agency contact and co-operation.

3. There was a need within districts to build up inter-agency contact and planning for all children. The development of coterminosity of boundaries for all agencies in Lothian will greatly enhance this inter-agency work.

4. There is inequality of provision in terms of number of places and choices of placement across Lothian region.

5. There is a need for the Social Work Department to be more actively involved in the planning of services for children aged 5–8 years.

6. Training in health care needs for daycare staff in relation to the integration of children with special needs, or specialist holiday support, have been identified, though funding for training will need to be identified.

The review process in relation to the Children Act has been a useful experience in providing an overview of the services available, the services which are deficient, and those that need development, and their distribution. Good practice was identified and the quality standards which have been developed for future registration and inspection of daycare services for subsequent reviews will hopefully lead to increasingly good quality daycare provision for children. Already deficiencies in provision and new developments needed have led to the setting up of appropriate inter-agency subgroups which will report back to the joint under eights liaison group, and hopefully lead to implementation.

In consolidating inter-agency work and joint responsibility for provision of good quality daycare it would be helpful if local district inter-agency teams could be closely involved in the initial part of the review process for services in their area, and recommendations for future developments. This will require time and commitment from all agencies.

It is critical to the review system that the quality standards agreed are acceptable, and realistically attainable so that in subsequent reviews they are seen as achievable goals rather than centrally imposed restrictions. It is anticipated that the review of standards in Lothian will continue to involve all relevant agencies.

East Lothian District, Sport and Recreation
Alan Murray

Early in July 1992 we were invited to comment, for the Under Eights Review, on the existing range of services and any gaps which we could identify within our district.

This inter-agency approach provided the opportunity to submit service details of activities and sessions undertaken in District Council-owned facilities and to remark on our perceived need, particularly for additional daycare facilities for both after school and holiday periods.

I consider that the communication arrangements between our respective departments was satisfactory, although in the first Review limited time was available to submit our response due to the tight timetable. Difficulties of this nature should not recur in future years.

One of the benefits arising from the Review was the information we gained on the detail and extent of service provided for the under eights in this district and also the opportunity we had to compare that service with other districts within Lothian Region. Such an exercise is valuable in reviewing service provision and focuses attention on the need for improvement. The duty to review on an inter-agency basis will in future years undoubtedly improve the corporate approach to service delivery.

It is evident that this Department's involvement in the service review was somewhat limited but in future years, with more time available, it is anticipated that our involvement and input would be of greater significance.

Lothian SPPA
Barbara Stirling

Early in 1992 SPPA Lothian was invited to meet with representatives from social Work, Education, the voluntary and private sectors along with members of the newly appointed Registration and Inspection Unit with the intention of harnessing the knowledge and skills of the agencies in the development of the document for standards for Part Day Group Care. SPPA Lothian welcomed the opportunity to contribute to this piece of work and recognised this as a positive approach by the local authority and a change in practice.

Further meetings were planned and a system drawn up whereby representatives checked out how the tasks could best be carried out within their own agency. In the case of SPPA this entailed reporting back to the Regional Executive Committee highlighting changes in legislation and practice; and the development of services which would now be required through introducing standards for all types of daycare.

Lothian Region welcomed SPPA having a Code of Practice and used it from time to time as a framework/reference when defining the standards indicators for Part Day Group Care. The Code of Practice is spelt out in the document as a reference for this particular standard.

This was an excellent piece of work between Social Work and SPPA Lothian which has helped to establish a close working relationship with Registration and Inspection It has given SPPA the opportunity to address other issues which have always been around but difficult to tackle even with a Code of Practice but without legislative backing. The introduction of standards now allows SPPA

Lothian to concentrate and focus on certain issues which are paramount when providing a good enough quality of care for young children and families.

SPPA Lothian recognised that the over-all response from playgroups in being re-registered is a positive one. There was a willingness to take on board any advice/recommendations put to them by the Registration Officer. However, at the same time this has great implications for our members (ie the playgroups) and the Association which does not have the financial means to support the groups through employing fieldworkers. This very important factor needs to be taken into account when raising the expectations of playgroups in Lothian through the Registration and Inspection visits. The Registration and Inspection Unit within the Social Work Department has a very clearly defined role but the support to playgroups is not so clearly defined and this is an issue which is currently being addressed by SPPA Lothian and the Region.

The consultation exercise and active participation in the beginning was very worthwhile. It reinforced the need for close liaison with similar agencies and the need for co-ordination and good planning to be included when taking any strategic overview of services.

Chapter 4

◆

BEING CONSULTED ON THE PROCESS

Throughout Scotland, as well as the larger more obvious agencies which were involved in the process, several smaller or more localised organisations were also consulted in the Review. Their responses indicate that, on the whole, they were satisfied with work they were able to do.

Fife Play Partnership
Joan Pennycook

In order to undertake the Section 19 Review as required under The Children Act, Fife Region had to create a consultative structure which did not previously exist. Access to information was restricted by the fact that no central database of information existed at that time.

The main consultative group was composed of representatives from the Social Work Department, the Education Department and the Health Board. They were responsible for drawing up the terms of reference and reaching agreement on the information required and the method of collection to be adopted. The critical factor effecting the review process was that of time, and other legislative demands to implement Section 10 of The Children Act at the same time. It is understood that this Review enabled a process to start bringing people together and getting mechanisms into place.

In order to create a central database of information the consultative group collected information by consulting with Under Eights Forums, the Scottish Childminding Association, and the Voluntary Sector Planning Liaison Group (Children and Families) under the umbrella of the Voluntary Organisations Regional Advisory Group whose members represent key organisations working with children and their families.

Having determined the format, content and consultation process for the Review, a period of two months was given for responses to the draft report. In order to consult as widely as possible with parents and carers of children under eight, 25,000 leaflets were distributed giving details about the purpose of the Review and informing them of access points for the general public to view the

Review report. The reverse of the leaflet was a questionnaire to be completed to assist in identifying gaps in services provided, evaluate existing services and in planning future services.

A total of 1000 copies of the report were distributed to organisations and public access points. Leaflets were distributed to parents and carers through primary schools, nurseries, playgroups and childminders. In addition, an advert was placed in local newspapers advising the public of where copies of the report were available.

Responses were received from thirteen organisations many of which commented on amendments, corrections and changes to the draft report. Of the 25,000 leaflets distributed, 2,157 were returned; a total response rate of 8.6%. The final report provides details of the breakdown of issues and services used. Unfortunately the figures for the 1991 Census were not available as these would have helped to make more sense of the results.

In general, voluntary organisations providing services to children under eight years of age in Fife acknowledge the difficulties faced by the local authority when undertaking the 1993 Review. Consultation with the voluntary sector prior to publishing the draft report was limited to the Scottish Pre-school Play Association, Scottish Childminding Association and the Voluntary Sector Planning Liaison Group.

The nature of the consultation was about data collection rather than providing an opportunity to participate in drawing up the terms of reference and determining the consultation process. Although a sub group was formed by the Voluntary Sector Planning and Liaison Group to meet with the Social Work Department to consider the consultative process for this and future reviews they met only once. To the regret of the group, the meeting concentrated on helping to fill gaps in the Social Work Department's knowledge of existing services and organisations and no further meeting has been convened.

There was a strong feeling that the process had already been agreed and the distribution channels agreed. It was more a matter of being kept informed rather than consulted. There are mixed feelings about whether or not comments for changes to specific entries or general aspects of the report were taken on board. For example, a request for changes to information about childminding were not made, but comments about the use of jargon did bring change.

The main thrust of consultation therefore was by distributing copies of the report to organisations and asking for responses within a two month period. On the whole this left many workers feeling dissatisfied with the consultative process overall but understanding of the difficulties involved. For some groups, other consultation issues were around at the same time and they were unable to respond to the Review report within the time limit.

Voluntary Sector workers are concerned that parents and carers were not greatly aware of the Review and what it was about, nor did they feel that on the whole the report was accessible. Large numbers of parents do not regularly use their local library or visit their GP, especially with young children, if using public transport. It is also considered highly unlikely that it reached the majority of parents and carers who do not use services or those only with children under 3 years.

Due to difficulties in targeting the public, consultation was directed at parents and carers already motivated to use a range of children's services. For example the Scottish Pre-school Play Association has easy access to parents, but they are only a particular type of group. This leaves a minority largely ignored.

The fact that leaflets and reports were printed only in English meant that Fife's ethnic communities, which constitute 1% of the total population, were not directly consulted or provided with opportunities to comment on their need for children's services in the future.

It is unclear, therefore, what the public as a whole got out of the Review. Organisations and Departments both in the statutory and voluntary sector have considerably more understanding of the context of the Review, but opinions would suggest that many of them are still unclear as the exact purpose of the Review. Is it just a source of information? What is its wider purpose? Responses received tended to concentrate on services not available or what they required in the future rather than commenting on the quality or otherwise of existing services.

There is no doubt that the Review report does provide an excellent reference of services available to parents and carers of children under eight years. Perhaps most importantly, the Review has provided the opportunity to open up dialogue between agencies and departments but this needs to be ongoing if it is to improve future inter-agency communications.

As yet the Social Work Department have been unable to look specifically at the issues raised from the questionnaire in terms of identifying gaps in services. This provides an excellent opportunity, if grasped, for the statutory, voluntary and private sectors to form an ongoing consultative group which would develop a co-ordinated approach to the development of children's services by valuing each others potential contribution.

The Scottish Pre-school Play Association in particular do feel that the consultation process has significantly affected the quality of their relationship with the Social Work Department at a higher level. So often, good communication exists between workers at grass roots level but they are powerless to create change. However, in broad terms, there is no evidence that indicates positive action to improve inter-agency communication is being taken; this may well require the consultation process for the 1995 Review to start again before any changes can take place.

It is understood that the consultative process has significantly affected inter-departmental awareness by highlighting the fact that different departments are developing parallel policies, indicating the need for a more co-ordinated approach to policy development of services for the under eights.

The duty on Local Authorities to Review services on a regular basis should increase the need to liaise with others. If undertaken meaningfully this should mean an improvement in communication both vertically and horizontally between agencies and departments. The expectations raised by the implementation of the Section 19 Review require to be followed through with some plan of action. If nothing happens Fife Region's high profile on children's services will lose credibility and the whole process will become pointless.

The pertinent question has been raised about what effect reorganisation of local authorities may have both on the process of consultation and the development of services.

- The consultation process needs to be ongoing and face to face with key people.
- The private sector need to be part of the consultative process as this is a growth area of service provision for child care.
- The voluntary sector needs to feel they are a real part of the process as often they work closest to users of services.
- If the consultation process is going to be right there needs to be a commitment to ensuring there is sufficient time to bring people together.
- There needs to be a close look at how to reach different sections of the community by tapping into key voluntary organisations, urban aid projects and community development projects.
- Key departments need to keep people informed at all stages.
- The consultation process must reach minority community groups.

The task of undertaking the Section 19 Review is a major one with lessons to be learned along the way. As long as people feel part of the process, are kept informed, understand the purpose fully and what can be expected as an outcome, the future Reviews should begin to fulfil their potential.

Grampian, SPPA
Jacky Barrett

SPPA were involved at the very outset of the review process when we were asked to serve on the Review Consultative Committee.

As SPPA's representative on the Committee it was my first opportunity to work alongside statutory and volunteer bodies in the child care sector. It was an illuminating experience. It constantly surprised me, especially as the only volunteer member, how involvement with SPPA had given me a broad knowledge of the pre-five sector, whilst some others were uncertain of the full range of services being provided. The reasons for this were many, but the main recommendation of the subsequent Review – that the departments should form a common policy on child care and establish better communication links – was arrived at very soon in the consultation process.

As a group, we soon established a close relationship, which was helped, I believe, by the standing of the people on the committee. I am not too sure, for instance, that I would have been as open about our own shortcomings if the people instrumental in whether we would be in receipt of a grant that year were sitting on the committee. By having such good communications, however, it was easy to quickly identify the main ideas for the Review document and be able to produce a document that contained most of the information we all felt was required. We were a little in the dark about the other processes going on – questionnaires etc – but Social Work felt these responses were confidential, so we didn't help evaluate them.

The interminable process of getting the final draft approved through committees was disheartening as it held up the printing and distribution – and when it was printed, so few copies were available (300?) that I doubt if it made the impact it probably should have done.

The consultation process did not take account of views of children themselves. This is difficult with under eights, but not impossible. Considering Grampian has endorsed the UN Convention, they should have tried to do this, I believe. Grampian has fallen into the same trap as most others – considering child care to be primarily an adult's need, not the child's.

The Review recommendation of setting up a joint consultative group was a good one, but lessons of the committee – more communication happens when less high-powered personnel are represented – have been ignored.

The seven areas identified to be tackled by the new Consultative Group are an interesting challenge – none of which can really be addressed without major funding implications. The suggestion in the document of looking anew at the use of resources is likely to be difficult as Grampian are committed to extending nursery education which leaves little room for major funding or for other provision.

There are already indications that agencies such as ourselves are going to be asked to be more professional and take on more responsibility – it is cost effective and the Council, by being our major grant source, has quite a lot of power to wield. However, by encouraging other types of provision – workplace nurseries, creches, after school clubs etc – there will be less adults around to run the playgroups that we support. It is a difficult balancing act that the Council has yet to recognise. SPPA exists to encourage and support parental involvement in the community run pre-school groups. If child care is encouraged by the Council to be handed over to "experts", then many of our groups, and maybe parts of our Association, will cease to function through lack of voluntary help.

The Review never took the step of addressing what Grampian's policy should be for the best care of children. This is a political minefield – it is hard to give major support to parental involvement and community groups whilst also supporting women returning to work and bucking the seemingly general view that education is best handled by paid professionals. In fact, political considerations were something which had to be taken into account – the first draft of the Review was far more radical in content.

The lesson SPPA learnt from the review process was that we worked in quite an insular way and didn't have the means to share resources with other agencies. In response to this, we are in the process of promoting a voluntary forum for agencies working with children. We hope the Council will support this forum as it could provide broad access to the non-statutory sector and enable agencies involved to promote their interests in a united way.

Reviews and implementation of the Children Act are going to be radically challenged by de-regionalisation. Grampian will no longer exist in a few years time, so it is important for non-statutory agencies to get their act together to ensure their voices continue to be heard and the Review is not forgotten. We have no indication how the next Review will be undertaken – I hope mechanisms have been put in place for collecting more accurate data after the frustrations experienced last time in trying to get all the information we felt was needed.

On a personal level, the Review was a real success. I made lots of valuable contacts and I know my voice was heard on behalf of SPPA. The problem is that I will not be around for the next Review (I'm only allowed 4 years on our Committee) and I suspect others are in the same situation. Personalities play a large part in the success of a team, and I hope the formal Consultative Group now in place will be able to achieve the same level of communication that existed in the first review process.

Overall, the Review in Grampian was good for SPPA as it highlighted the important part that playgroups play in child care provision. We were consulted about Grampian's own guidelines to the Act and have raised our profile considerably over the past year through the contacts made. Whether we can maintain this momentum is a challenge for ourselves and the Council. We know we are a major resource and hopefully the Council will continue to recognise this.

One Plus Strathclyde
John Findlay

To review the range of services for under eights in a Region the size of Strathclyde was a massive task to undertake given the limited time available. One Plus as an organisation was anxious to take part in this process because the development of accessible, affordable and high quality childcare provision is a central component to our campaigning activities. The lack of childcare available for both pre and school age children means that access to training, further education, employment and activities is denied to many lone parents. For the first time, the Review offered the opportunity to identify and assess the range of childcare services on offer across Strathclyde Region.

There were a number of avenues through which voluntary organisations could represent their views to pre-five services. The main one being through the Strathclyde Early Years Voluntary Sector Forum. One Plus has been involved in the Forum since its inception in 1986 to provide a formal link between the Pre-five Committee, the Education Department and the voluntary sector in Strathclyde. After the draft Review document was published in October 1992, a seminar was organised by Strathclyde Early Years Forum and the Pre-fives Services as part of the consultation process. The aim of the seminar was:

- to respond to the regional document and make voluntary organisations aware of the divisional reviews taking place;
- to stimulate voluntary organisations interest in the Review and encourage their involvement in the consultation process.

The seminar organised by SEYF enabled One Plus and other voluntary organisations to play a part in the review process. As with any consultation process and in particular one that has taken place for the first time, there was room for improvement. In particular:

- the timescale imposed by the requirement to produce the first Review meant that the consultation period was fairly short (7 weeks) after the publication of the draft Review;
- this constraint was particularly important in trying to consult with locally based community organisations.

Nevertheless, the consultation process was fairly wide ranging and a genuine attempt to involve a large cross section of childcare providers.

The Review itself highlighted a number of very important issues in relation to the range in quality of services provided for the under eights. Particularly welcome was the recognition of both the role played by the voluntary sector in providing childcare and the concept of equal partnership in the development of services. From the voluntary sector's view the major issues which arose from the Review were:

i) The uneven development of services throughout Strathclyde clearly highlighted the ad hoc way that development of services to under eights had taken place. In some areas of Strathclyde pre-five services were provided in the main by the voluntary sector.

ii) The Review contained a mass of information regarding services to under eights. However, there was little in the way of qualitative information regarding the provision of services, and in the different role of, and approaches taken by the different types of provision, eg child and family centres, nursery schools, nursery centres, creches, childminders. It would have been interesting to explore the interaction between what each type of service has to offer, and any overlap between them.

iii) The Review document outlines the regional council's admissions policy. However, again it would have been useful to have had some information regarding the numbers of children who are allocated places from each of the different bandings, the operation of admissions policies etc.

iv) The needs of parents and children from the ethnic minority community, while recognised, are not discussed in any detail within the Review document. Information regarding the proportion of children from the ethnic minority community who use the childcare services on offer and any barriers which may exist to their involvement would be important in assessing the input of equal opportunities policies and operation of the admissions policy.

v) The financial situation facing local authorities has meant that the resources committed to funding voluntary organisations have not grown in recent years and have often failed to keep pace with inflation. However, the Children Act has increased the responsibilities of childcare providers in terms of registration and information procedures. To meet this, voluntary organisations have had to devote more resources and time to this area which has not been matched by an increase in funding.

vi) Linked to the funding issues is the need to raise the quality of service provided through training for staff, volunteers and committee members. The pressures of funding mean that it is becoming increasingly difficult to maintain the service and to enable staff/volunteers to attain their proper training level. It is always a difficult balance for voluntary organisations, made worse by the squeeze on funding.

vii) The information on out of school care schemes was very welcome, but as with the pre-five services, the uneven development over the Region was highlighted.

The Children Act 1989 was a significant step in recognising the need to develop high quality services which meet the needs of parents. The Review itself is a key element of this process and enabled a wide range of different interests to have an input in the debate about the future of childcare services. The Review Document provides a mass of information which was previously unavailable, and provides a basis for local authorities, voluntary organisations and other childcare providers to work in partnership in developing a range of childcare services for the 0–8 age range. Nevertheless, a tension still exists between the level of current need, the provision of a high quality service available to all sections of the community and the level of resources currently available. For the 75% of lone parents in Strathclyde living at Income Support Levels, reviewing childcare service, whilst important in itself, does little to enable them to escape the poverty trap without increasing the levels of real resources devoted to developing new childcare provision.

Stepping Stones in Scotland
Anne Lancaster

Stepping Stones in Scotland was asked to provide a representative on one of the two working groups set up by Strathclyde Regional Council to focus on aspects of implementation of the Children Act. Representation on the Review Procedures working group added a family centre perspective to the work and, additionally, as the organisation was the only voluntary sector representative, a voluntary sector perspective.

The level of involvement and consultation with Stepping Stones in Scotland throughout the review process was good with draft copies of all the implementation papers being sent to the organisation. An additional possibility to input into the process was provided by a joint Strathclyde Early Years Voluntary Sector Forum (SEYVSF)/ Strathclyde Regional Council conference (chaired by the Stepping Stones in Scotland Director). At regional level the degree of involvement of the voluntary sector was very satisfactory, facilitated to a large extent by the presence of SEYVSF which already had good working links with the Regional Council.

The main benefit was in having the opportunity to influence the Review document. It also gave an insight into how important different people's perspectives could be in influencing the outcome of the work. For example, problems arose in completing registration documents. These were due in the main to the fact that the voluntary sector representation on that working group came from organisations concerned with childminding and playgroups. The documents produced as a result of the group's work reflected those needs and were appropriate only for these two types of provision – which provide the majority of daycare services. However, this caused enormous difficulties for other types of provision including creches and family centres. The problem was raised with the Council at Divisional level with little success, but, when taken up at Regional level through SEYVSF, the problems were addressed.

Like many other voluntary agencies Stepping Stones in Scotland saw the publication of the Review as an opportunity for working with local authorities towards identifying and filling gaps in provision, and examining quality issues. The advent of restructured local government within three years makes this exercise difficult to begin because of the uncertainties around who will be providing services for young families in the future, how they will be funded and how many of the non-statutory services will survive the transitional period.

Cothrom Centre, South Uist, Western Isles
Mary MacInnes

The consultation of childcare services by the Social Work Department of the Western Isles Council heightened my awareness as to the lack of services the Council provides. No nursery schools or classes exist and pre-school provision outside the town of Stornoway relies on the efforts of volunteers involved in setting up and running playgroups and mother and toddler groups.

Playgroups, in some cases, are listed as being bi-lingual although no explanation is given as to what "bi-lingual" means.

The document produced can only be seen as a list of facilities and contacts, giving only the minimum of information about playgroups. Like most lists this one is out of date before it arrives from the printers!

I am disappointed that the training of carers and childcare provision being experimented with at Cothrom's Centre in Stoneybridge is only listed like any other Gaelic playgroup. Although it is noted that Cothrom was consulted when the consultation document was being written no-one within the organisation recalls being consulted.

Primrosehill Living Training Resource
Frances Littlejohn

I am employed by Aberlour Child Care Trust which manages a Family Centre, incorporating a training resource, in a designated area of Aberdeen. For almost two years we have been actively involved in promoting the Guidelines for Implementation of Part X of the Children Act 1989 and have used the standards recommended in the guidelines as a basis for discussion and training sessions with a wide variety of groups in the designated areas of Aberdeen city.

Our Urban Aid project has a remit to improve the quality of child care in the designated areas of the city. We therefore felt, given our working knowledge of childcare in those areas, that it would be both useful and appropriate to request a consultation with the officer appointed to oversee Grampian Regional Council's first review of daycare services for under eights.

The development officer subsequently visited our project in June 1992 when I had the opportunity to raise with her a number of issues and concerns.

Our experiences with local child care groups had highlighted the following:

• The very groups which benefit most by giving consideration to the standards were going to be ignored by the registration process. Many of the groups we support, i.e. creches and out of school provision, often operate for a maximum of two hours at a time, and are therefore not required to register under the terms of the Act.

- Many groups perceived the registration process as a threat to their existence because of the requirements of the Firemaster and Environmental Health Department.
- Adult Education and Community Education budgets did not allow for adequate resourcing of creche provision.

Based on the above we felt we were in a position to contribute to the consultation process and offer some of our own suggestions for prioritising and paving the way forward in Grampian.

These are harnessed in the following benefits:

- That the spirit of the Act, and the guidelines relating to the standards, provided a benchmark against which all child care could be evaluated.
- That all children are entitled to certain standards of care and all those working with children are entitled to equal respect for their work - irrespective of contact time.
- That **all** childcare should be given the same status and that a Region wide commitment to the spirit of the Act should demonstrate that creches and out of school care groups are very much on the agenda. Only by doing this could we hope to improve the quality of service on offer to all our children.
- That additional resources allocated be to allow groups to comply with the standards.
- That the registration process should highlight and prioritise the quality of the human interaction in childcare settings rather than focusing on the physical space, e.g. quantity of toilets, etc.
- That there needs to be an ongoing collaborative inter-agency approach to the review process which includes the parental perspective and those childcare groups operating in the community.
- That if women are to have equal access to training opportunities then this needs to be reflected in realistic funding for creches.
- That childcare workers from a range of settings should have access to training which reflects the needs of parents and children and their own professional development.

Intrinsically linked to the above we wanted to see mechanisms in place to ensure that the profile of childcare issues which had been highlighted by the review process would continue to be on everyone's agenda.

In this context our own Policy and Monitoring Group wrote to Grampian Region's Joint Consultative Group which was convened in March 1993 to consider the issues identified in the Review document. As a local voluntary childcare organisation we were seeking representation on the group, but to date (September 1993) we have not yet had a reply.

In conclusion, I would like to congratulate the officer whose responsibility it was to produce Grampian's first Review document. Given the constraints of time and accepting that it was a "starting point" I felt that many of the issues which we felt important had been represented fairly in chapter five of the Review. Feedback from some of the groups who contacted Grampian Regional Council's Under Eights Department in connection with the registration process has been positive on the whole, demonstrating that the department is using its discretion in a pragmatic way.

Our hope is that the momentum generated by the first Review is not lost, and that the process of consultation continues and develops into a "Grampian Children's Forum" which would lead to a marked improvement in collaboration, not only between Education and Social Work departments, but between all individuals and agencies concerned with the quality and quantity of resources and services for families with young children.

CONCLUSION

It was the intention in commissioning work for this book to try to obtain as wide a perspective as possible on how Scotland's first Review of services for under eights was conducted and what it could mean for the development of services for early years.

The review process itself, in five of Scotland's local authorities, has been examined through descriptions and analysis of the work by lead officers from these authorities. Local politicians who have an interest in the political implications of the duty to review have also expressed their views. In addition, many of the other agencies, either involved in the process or consulted on the draft documents, have commented on their perceptions of the value of the Review and the opportunities it presents for developments in inter-agency working and service development. What appears is therefore a reflection of the experience of those involved both in carrying out the reviews and through consultation.

It emerges that there is wide recognition that the duty to review represents a major opportunity to raise the profile of early years work, to raise its position on the political agenda, to use the information gathered for the Review to make improvements in the way services are targeted and to examine ways in which organisations can work together to provide better services.

However, there is also a view, overwhelmingly expressed, that the value of the Review and its ability to influence service development at a local level depends very heavily on a response in policy and resources teams, from the national government. It has been repeatedly pointed out that, unless The Scottish Office and central government use the information contained in the Reviews to alter policies on public funding of childcare, the effect of the duty to review, in service development terms, can only be of a limited nature largely confined to considerations of how best to target existing resources.

Nevertheless, the Children Act legislation as it applies in Scotland has been widely welcomed and local authorities, despite all the problems associated with the first Review, have all made honest and strenuous efforts to carry through their obligations under the Act and to take a constructive view of the value of the exercise.

The work has not been without its complications for some authorities. Where the previous early years infrastructure could not cope with the demands of the Review, the exercise required fundamental thinking on creating appropriate inter-agency structures to carry out the work. The Review has therefore led to change in local authorities which may turn out to have far reaching effects in the way agencies work together to deliver services for young children. This collaborative approach to delivering services for early years has been generally welcomed, although, inevitably, there have been problems associated with forming new relationships and coming to common understandings.

COMMON FEATURES OF THE REVIEWS ACROSS SCOTLAND

Time Scale

All Reviews, including those not examined in this book, made explicit concerns about the time scale given in which to complete the task and the effect this had, both on the quality of information which could be produced and the extent to which it was possible to consult with other agencies and providers and users of services.

Resources

Most Reviews, in describing the processes engaged in to carry out the Review, evidenced the lack of resources available to do the work. Few authorities appointed extra staff. Any funding used for the Reviews came from diverting money from other budgets within the local authorities. There was no funding made available for this work from The Scottish Office. Even so, much to their credit, all authotities have produced detailed Reviews providing a wealth of information on early years services in Scotland.

Scope of the Review

All Reviews acknowledged that the first attempt must, of necessity, be limited to an audit of the amount of provision available with little consideration of the quality of that provision. Most authorities also attempted to look at gaps in provision shown up by the Review process and to bring to the fore some of the issues highlighted. Several Reviews also went on to make recommendations as to how to begin to address those issues.

However, there was a degree of uncertainty, either expressed or implicit, in the Reviews as to how to use the information they contain or how to pursue the issues they threw up. Some Reviews contained explicit recommendations without identifying clear pathways for their implementation. Other Reviews resulted in the construction of Review groups with a remit to consider the implications and recommendations of the Review. One Review simply listed the services available, though with a clear indication that future reviews would consider wider issues identified by the Review process. In spite of these uncertainties, there was general recognition that the Review was more than a snapshot of provision in time, and should be viewed as a continuous process with triennial reports detailing progress.

Overseeing the Review

Groups brought together across Scotland for the purpose of overseeing the Reviews had different complexions reflecting particular local circumstances and pre-existing structures as well as the creation of new ones. They all involved organisations other than the Social Work and Education Departments. However, only one local authority (Tayside) managed to achieve representation on its overseeing body from parents.

All authorities were required to ensure the involvement of local council members. The extent to which they achieved this varied across Scotland. It is evident from contributions made by members to this book that there was considerably less involvement in small rural and island authorities than in the larger authorities with major centres of population. The reasons for this have been identified by members themselves and include geographical difficulties, preoccupation with other major legislation and expenses. However, greater involvement in the process appears to have contributed to greater understanding of the purpose of the Review and its potential for influencing the future development and range of service provision. Greater clarity over the purpose of member involvement and the extent of involvement by members would enhance the effectiveness of the Review. Without member involvement and understanding the ability of the Review to influence policy development and strategic planning is limited.

Carrying out the Review

All authorities across Scotland delegated the work of co-ordinating the Review to lead officers within Social Work and Education Departments. Most of these were already in posts with much wider job remits, although a few authorities appointed new staff to Social Work Departments and some Education Departments had to second or appoint staff specifically to work with colleagues in Social Work.

Most authorities brought together teams of people who gathered together the information. All involved colleagues in the voluntary sector and other agencies such as the Health Boards to some degree. The way in which these teams worked and the degree of delegation to agencies outside Social Work and Education varied and seemed to depend largely on how well developed working relationships across agencies were before the Review.

INFORMATION IN THE REVIEWS

Starting Points

From the evidence presented in previous chapters, Review teams, in their attempts to gather together the basic information required started with what they knew already, using the registration and inspection data bases on childcare providers. For some authorities this provided virtually complete information on all registerable provision. For other authorities, where the registration process had been slower to get off the ground there were gaps in this information. For nearly all authorities, the information available on provision for school-aged children up to eight years was incomplete.

Standardisation and National Use of Statistics

Beyond the information on registerable provision and that provided by the local authority through their own services, information was not available in any systematic or standard form and so what has appeared in the Reviews varies considerably from authority to authority across Scotland. Decisions as to what to include and what not to include seem to have been made on an idiosyncratic and individual basis from authority to authority.

The way in which the information was collected, collated, ordered and then presented also varied between the various authorities so that it is almost impossible to make meaningful direct statistical comparisons across the Reviews. Since one of the major elements of importance attached to the Reviews has to be to inform future policy at a national level it is important for information to be collected and presented in a standardised way so that national trends and issues emerge and The Scottish Office has access to directly comparable statistical information across all local authorities. (As was clearly expressed by the Lothian Review, there is a need for "identification of national themes and trends, reconciliation of disparate approaches to providing for under-eights – a framework within which resources can be allocated effectively".) Work has already begun on reaching agreement on the proper extent of the development of national guidelines for the gathering and presentation of data for the Review.

What is required is a systematic and standardised approach which will facilitate policy development nationally. However, even nationally coherent statistics from local authorities will be of limited value to The Scottish Office if up to date national statistics are not more readily available.

Dissemination of Information

At a local level a number of the Reviews in Scotland were also concerned that there was not an adequate free flow of information across agencies and departments. This led to inefficiencies, duplication of effort and consequently a service, some aspects of which such as training, were not well targeted. There was recognition, in respect of training at least, that better information sharing across departments and with the voluntary sector would lead to wider access and better take up.

Similarly, several Reviews recognised that there was a need for a better information service on early years facilities for potential users. A number of Reviews indicated their intentions to package the information gathered in a form which the users would have easy access to. However, only two of the Reviews explicitly identified the need for this information to be available in the main ethnic minority languages.

MEMBERS' INVOLVEMENT AND POLICY DEVELOPMENT
Structures

The Scottish Office guidelines on the Review made it clear that it should be conducted on a collaborative basis and that there should be political involvement in the form of elected member guidance.

Local authorities throughout Scotland made widely differing arrangements for this, largely reflecting conditions pertaining in each region prior to the Children Act. As described in earlier chapters, Strathclyde and Lothian used existing joint sub-committees of Social Work and Education to oversee the process. Grampian, although it also had a joint sub-committee, set up a Review Consultative Committee. Borders used its Member/Officer Early Years Advisory Group,

For some local authorities the duty to review highlighted a lack of any structures and so it acted as a catalyst for an increase in inter-departmental collaboration – Dumfries and Galloway set up a joint sub-committee, Tayside set up a Regional Under Eights Co-ordinating Group and Orkney has established a joint sub-committee.

In other regions, e.g. Highland, it was officers of the Social Work and Education Departments who steered the work with the role of members being limited to considerations of draft and final reports. This trend was particularly evident in the smaller rural and island authorities.

Degree of Involvement

The level of member involvement, even in those authorities where there were joint sub-committees established, was generally limited. Constraints seem to have centred on a number of issues:

- the short time scale of the Review
- problems of geographical distance and consequent cost of attending meetings in northern and island regions
- the burden of other major legislative change e.g. in community care, local government reorganisation, devolved management of schools.
- uncertainty as to what a member's role could be without stepping into an officer role

Benefits of Involvement

As Chapter 2 convincingly shows, members generally felt that the Review has major implications for the development of corporate policies and strategies, for inter-agency working and for service development. There was general acceptance that the role of members needed to be considered and clarified before the nest Review so that the benefits of involvement would be fully exploited.

It is obvious from reports in Chapter 2 that the benefits of involvement are recognised by members and include:

- a greater understanding of the importance of early years services
- a greater understanding of the needs of local communities
- an ability to make policy decisions based on a secure knowledge base
- an aid to corporate planning of services through collaboration across departments and committees
- a raising of the profile of early years work

Members' Concern

Whilst the benefits were accepted, members voiced concern about the future of early years work based on the observation that service development opportunities will depend on proper resourcing and this will be extremely difficult at a time when the central government is not making any particular financial assistance available for early years work.

Equally, there is concern that local government reorganisation will affect, as least in the short term, local authorities' ability to consider service development needs and will provide a disruption to the long term planning process.

Local Policy Development

The involvement of elected members in the Review process has far reaching implications for the development of policy – policy devised by elected members in collaboration with officers will direct strategic planning and must, in turn, be informed by the Review process itself. Several Reviews pointed up the need for clear policy frameworks for early years work but it is evident that for many authorities the policy framework is not there! In addition, it is clear that the Children Act and the Review process itself are encouraging a corporate approach to the provision of services. Policies will therefore require to be developed in most local authorities in a framework which will allow a collaborative response, not just in the statutory sector but including the voluntary and private sectors.

National Policy Development

Policy development at a local level, although vital, will not be enough. Concern was expressed in a few of the Reviews that the process itself, particularly the public elements of consultation, had raised expectations that attempts would be made to fill the gaps identified by the process. However, there was general recognition that, in most cases, this would not be possible without a change in policy direction at a national level which would enable fresh injections of resources.

The information presented by the Reviews across Scotland shows very clear and consistent gaps in provision eg for ethnic minorities, for rural communities, for children during out of school hours. This information, gathered for the first time right across Scotland, presents The Scottish Office with an important opportunity, along with local authorities and others, to consider the level of resources it allocates and how best to target these resources so that those groups currently with the least services benefit. A national examination of the Reviews and consideration of their implications for both national and local policy development and resource allocation may enable service development in local authorities which provides a better targeted and more comprehensive service.

POLICY DEVELOPMENT AND INTER-AGENCY WORK

Roots of Policy

A few Reviews stated that their roots for policy frameworks were firmly fixed in the UN Convention on the Rights of the Child. Since the Convention places the child at the centre and considers responsibilities towards that child based on certain fundamental rights, it would seem a logical place from which to derive a basic philosophy, and key fundamental principles to underpin policy development. Putting the child and his/her developmental needs at the centre would also encourage the sort of co-ordinated response which the Children Act and Review process itself are trying to achieve.

It is central to the Children Act that the child comes first and that the child's developmental needs must be placed at the centre of the providers' responses to meeting those needs. This inevitably means a blurring of the distinct lines of difference between the care of the child and the education of the child. The Children Act works against the clear delineation of difference between the two and essentially suggests that the dichotomy is a false one. This has clear implications for the shape of future childcare policy and the ways in which agencies and departments work together.

A co-ordinated approach to policy

All Reviews in Scotland recognise that clear policies based on a co-ordinated approach are central to the development of a coherent and comprehensive service for young children.

A few local authorities already had a corporate policy framework through which they operated though these tended only to involve local authority departments rather than all providers of services. However, as Tayside states in its Review, "in making the most efficient use of scarce resources, a co-ordinated policy with joint planning opportunities is essential".

Partnership

The major benefit of the Reviews is recognised by all authorities to have been the encouragement to inter-agency working – the forging and strengthening of relationships across departments and agencies so that there is, in several cases for the first time, a real sense that work will begin to move forward on a partnership basis involving all sectors. This is recognised as being particularly important at a time when resources are severely limited and local authorities can no longer realistically expect to expand services significantly without working in partnership with others.

Some authorities have considerably further to go than others in developing a co-ordinated response to provision for young children. Several authorities already have a tradition of Social Work and Education Departments and sometimes Health Boards working in partnership, but few authorities have gone so far as to develop working relationships with the voluntary and private sectors based on equality and a far reaching collaboration on service development. This is true even when it is conceded by the local authority, as it is in Highland Region and other particularly rural authorities, that the voluntary sector is the major provider. However, there is growing recognition of the importance of the partnership approach. As Strathclyde stated in their Review: "There should be active co-ordination of services at a local level and voluntary organisations and community groups should be treated as equal partners in the provision of services." It is interesting to note, in this respect, that Strathclyde, despite its size, appears to have found it relatively easy to begin implementing the Review, because of its already highly developed inter-agency structures, as clearly demonstrated in Chapter 2.

Differing Perspectives

Several authorities recognise that the Review has "pioneered co-operative approaches to planning and delivering of services for this age group" (Tayside), and the process, now it has begun, will continue. However, it is also clear that the process of collaboration must acknowledge that the perspectives of agencies involved will differ, along with the emphasis they will put on particular services. Any co-ordinated planning framework will need to be based on a reconciliation of these differences to form a joint philosophy under-pinning policy development in early years services.

Shape of Service Development

For several authorities the creation of a co-ordinated framework may suggest the need for a re-examination of organisational and departmental structures, since it implies a degree of inter-agency working across all departments and sectors which may lead to a blurring of traditional areas of responsibility, and a questioning of departmental roles and functions. Interdisciplinary working on a collaborative basis cannot be achieved without a degree of open-mindedness and certain willingness to give up traditional "power bases" for the sake of a better integrated, better quality more coherent service better suited to meeting the needs of children.

If agencies are to make a truly collaborative response across the disciplines then the shape of the services provided for young children will alter and many innovative ways of providing services become possible which are not viable in the present context. The issue of whether an inter-agency response will lead to a more efficient way of providing services which better meet the needs of local communities is one which local authorities need to explore as they look at ways of working together. It is encouraging that the Reviews indicate an acceptance of the need for co-ordinated policy frameworks and a willingness to work with other agencies to achieve this.

CONSULTATION

The Scottish Office guidelines on the Review required the lead officers in Social Work and Education to involve and consult with a wide range of agencies and organisations operating in the early years field, including Health Boards, voluntary organisations, other local authority departments, the private sector and parents.

Key Organisations

Some of the contributions in Chapter 2 would seem to indicate that for some authorities it was relatively easy to arrange involvement of key organisations since they already had well established relationships with them through voluntary sector fora, planning groups and liaison meetings illustrating the value of such inter-agency groupings. For other authorities these structures needed to be set up and new relationships forged.

On the whole, major agencies such as the Scottish Pre-school Play Association and the Scottish Childminding Association seem to have been reasonably satisfied with the degree to which they were involved in the Review process, though there are criticisms to be made concerning feelings that they were not taken sufficiently seriously, at least in the initial phases.

Other Major Agencies

In general terms, the collective approach to the Review seems to have been a very rewarding and positive experience for those involved. However, there were problems associated with the consultation. It seems, for example, to have been difficult for some authorities, where there was not a tradition of collaborative working, to ascertain the views of the Health Board staff in any systematic way. Where Health Board staff were involved, however, they seem to have viewed it as a useful experience, recognising, as the contribution from both Lothian and Borders Health Boards illustrated, the link between the availability of a good quality child care service and the healthy development of children.

Equally, it seems to have been difficult in some authorities to gain the views of other local authority departments with, perhaps, a less obvious interest in services for young children. Very few authorities seem to have enlisted the involvement of Planning or Chief Executive's Departments and most District Council Leisure and Recreation Departments do not seem to have been involved to any significant degree. Since any strategy for an integrated service must take account of the total child environment it will be important to involve these agencies in the next Review.

The Public and Parents

As earlier chapters illustrate, all local authorities made strong attempts to consult with a very wide range of bodies and individuals including parents. The measures they adopted varied from region to region, but included radio and newspaper coverage, public meetings, questionnaires and street interviews. All Reviews highlighted the difficulties in carrying out consultation exercises and particularly expressed disappointment in the responses they had had from the general public and direct providers of services.

Problems of consultation in rural areas were exacerbated by the problem of meaningfully getting the views of a scattered population when geographical distance often made attendance at open meetings impossible. This was particularly the case in Highland Region although it was considered by others too. Lothian spoke for many other authorities when it stated in its Review: "The process highlighted the lack of adequate channels through which meaningful consultation should take place."

Responses to questionnaires and attendances at public meetings had been, in the main, poor. However, three authorities, particularly, managed to achieve more successful consultations with the public and parents and a number of factors particular to these authorities emerge as having contributed to their success. These include:

1. The Reviews being part of a much bigger and more thorough going Review designed to inform policy development, which has been sufficiently resourced to be meaningful – Central Region.
2. The Review being carried out in an area with a high level of provision and a high political and public profile for services for children and families – Fife Region.
3. The consultation taking the innovative form of a series of street interviews – Dumfries and Galloway Region.

These consultations were the exception. If the Review is to be an accurate reflection of both the level and standard of provision and what users actually think of it, adequate consultation is essential and innovative ways must be found of facilitating these.

Form of future consultation

Despite general disappointment over the level of response, for most authorities consultation served a highly useful purpose in helping to identify issues of concern and ensuring that they receive priority in agendas for future discussions in local authorities on where effort should go in the development of services.

However, it would be useful for local authorities to decide what form consultation for future Reviews should take, and particularly to consider how wide the consultation should be. It may make sense, for example, not to try to achieve blanket coverage, but to find a way of representative sampling.

It would also be useful for local authorities to consider carefully at what stage in the Review process and to what purpose they consult with people and organisations. Is it sensible to consult once a full draft report is available, or should the consultation take the form of an examination of the major issues, drawn from the basic statistical information, at an interim stage in the Review process? In that way, the results of the consultation could be fully and properly incorporated in the Review document and fundamentally influence its shape. It would be useful for local authorities to share ideas on these questions and find ways to consult effectively, though local differences will mean that there cannot be a nationally definitive answer.

It is encouraging that there is a commitment, expressed in several of the Reviews, to improve consultation procedures for the next Review and particularly to look at meaningful ways of gaining the views of parents and, in some instances, children themselves. Fife, particularly, has expressed a desire and a commitment to consult with children for the next Review. They would certainly have some valid things to say, for example, about out of school care.

As earlier chapters show, consultation is recognised as an important aid to the evaluation of current services, the assessment of quality and the verification of the relationship of local services to the needs of local communities. It merely remains to find an effective means of doing it.

EFFECTIVENESS IN RELATING TO PARTICULAR GROUPS

It could have been expected that all the Reviews would have considered the ways in which they delivered services to certain groups with a community of interest e.g. children with special needs, children from ethnic minorities, rural children and single parent families.

Children with Special Needs

All Reviews in Scotland listed the services available for this diverse group of children. Several authorities also appeared to be considering the types and levels of services required as part of the wider Community Care plans. Several authorities made it clear in their Reviews that they were aware of inadequacies in the services offered in their region and in particular showed concern to improve on inter-agency co-ordination and support for families. It is clear that most local authorities are not properly acquainted with the full range of children with special needs within their areas and do not have a fully integrated service across Health, Education and Social Work in both the public and independent sectors.

However, a number of authorities explicitly recognised in the Review that the two guiding principles which should lie behind their response to children with special needs concerned a recognition of the needs of the child as a child first and any special needs as part of the character of that child and a corresponding need to integrate that child with children in the wider community as far as was possible. Even so, it is a matter of serious concern that, when no new resources have been allocated to local authorities, there is no duty to provide services implicit in those parts of the Children Act applicable in Scotland, and with the delay in the White Paper through parliament, these children will continue to struggle to have their needs met.

Children from Ethnic Minorities

The Reviews in general were characterised by a lack of information about this group of children, although it was apparent that the services they were aware of were not meeting the needs. Few authorities in Scotland made any strong and deliberate attempt to consult with people from ethnic minorities to gain their views on services. Only one, Central Region, appears to have had some success. What emerged from that consultation was a severe lack of awareness of services available on the part of ethnic minority communities, coupled with a desire to use services, but with a stipulation that they must be sensitive to the discrete cultural and linguistic requirements of ethnic minorities. It also seemed that there was a desire for services, childminders particularly, which came from within ethnic minority communities themselves.

From this consultation people from ethnic minorities it appears, do not have enough trust in the existing provision and are interested in developing services of their own. The issues for local authorities from this one aspect of the consultative process would seem to indicate a need to consider:

- how best to make information available other than simply publishing it in appropriate languages, helpful though that is;

- how to make sure that all existing provision takes account of different cultural needs and there is a better understanding of the implications of implementing equal opportunities policies;

- how to encourage people from ethnic minorities to develop childcare facilities within their communities.

There appears to have been little attempt through the Review to look, in a systematic way, at the requirements in terms of services for these groups. The Reviews have highlighted a situation which appears to stem from poor communication between local authority departments, particularly, and community groups set up around issues affecting ethnic minorities. It is encouraging that several Reviews recognise their failure in this respect and have indicated their intention to make building links with these groups a priority.

Rural Families

Although all authorities in Scotland have rural communities within their boundaries not all recognise rural families as having particular needs separate from those of the general population. Some authorities did not make mention of rural families at all in their reviews, including some with significant rural populations.

Of those that did recognise the particular needs of children in rural areas the main concern centred around lack of services and the need to try to achieve a "parity of treatment" in comparison with children who lived in towns. In one authority (Highland Region) this was held to mean greater support for the playgroup movement rather than an increase in local authority provision, due to the proportionately greater costs in making, eg, nursery education available in small rural schools. However, it is encouraging to note that one of the few areas where there has been an increase in provision resulting from the Review has been in Tayside where, as mentioned in Chapter 2, two new posts have been created in rural districts to support the District Forum.

The fact that rural children were not given any particular attention in a significant number of the Reviews is evidence that the needs of rural families are not being recognised as being qualitatively different from those of urban families. This is exacerbated in the regions where the emphasis of local authority effort is placed on urban areas of multiple deprivation to the detriment of services in rural areas. Future Reviews will need to look more closely at the particular requirements of rural families. Hopefully, this will be facilitated by improved consultative procedures which all local authorities indicated in the Reviews they hoped to have in place for the next Review.

One parent families

Virtually the only references in any of the Reviews throughout Scotland concerning single parent families were contained in socio-economic data as part of the context for the Review. The only other mention made in some Reviews was related to poverty indicators and concerned single parents' need for childcare in relation to employment and training opportunities. It was recognised that demand for daycare at an affordable price for this group far outstripped supply.

Few Reviews made explicit the need for better support services for single parent families. It would seem that this group is not being given priority in consideration of services and its needs do not appear to be being recognised in any explicit and coherent way. Again, this is a situation which may improve once better consultation procedures are in place in time for the next Review.

Future strategies for services for special interest groups

It is undoubtedly the case that there are particular groups in the community who are ill served under current service provision arrangements. The Review has highlighted this and it is now up to local authorities in consultation with other interested organisations to establish the basic links with groups which will allow them to gain access to the sort of information which will be essential if an appropriate response in terms of service provision is to be made.

Most Reviews signalled an intention to begin this process as a matter of priority. The Children Act Review has, by allowing organisations and agencies to work together, given new insights into gaps in provision and issues which need to be addressed. It must also bring agencies together in a partnership which will consider seriously how to develop and resource a service for young children which will meet the real needs of children and families in all their diverse forms.

QUALITY AND TRAINING

Quality Standards

There is a clear recognition in all the Reviews throughout Scotland that the issue of quality has not been tackled first time around and there is an obvious need to consider it in future Reviews.

Comment, both within the Reviews and by interested organisations, has recognised the difficulties in considering quality provision since it inevitably leads to discussion as to what constitutes quality – a value laden concept. This discussion is not a new one. There have already been several useful contributions to the debate from such organisations as the EC Childcare Network. However, if the Review is to fulfil one of its primary functions, which is to raise the standards of childcare available to children, it would be beneficial for there to be nationally agreed quality standards against which provision could be measured. These standards need to be developed alongside the debate and take account of and have respect for such differences as are brought about by different cultural perspectives.

Application of standards

The problem of applying such standards, of course, raises the question of what to do where particular facilities do not achieve them. Would raising standards inevitably lead to closing down some childcare and could that be considered a positive development, when, as has already been seen in the system, current levels of provision nowhere near meet demand?

Equally, is it right to impose quality standards on child care providers when it is not likely that there will be the support mechanisms or training opportunities available to providers to realistically enable the majority of them to reach those standards? As was pointed out by Pat Jackson of Lothian Health Board in an earlier contribution: "It is critical to the Review system that the quality standards agreed are acceptable and realistically attainable so that in the subsequent reviews they are seen as achievable goals rather than centrally imposed restrictions."

Training

Nearly all Reviews recognised that training opportunities were insufficient within their areas. Concern was expressed particularly at the lack of opportunities for training in working with children with special needs, child development, child protection and equal opportunities. These questions raise fundamental issues which local authorities must address when considering the question of raising standards and how to support providers towards attaining them.

As all Reviews in Scotland recognised, there is not sufficient investment in training in childcare despite its obvious link with quality care and the status of childcare work. Until recently, there were not even any nationally recognised qualifications in childcare other than college based SCOTVEC courses leading to SNNB registration. This was remedied with the launch of SVQs in Childcare and Education, widely recognised in the Review as being of major importance. However, the progress of implementation of these qualifications has been slow. The major obstacle being the considerable cost to candidates, considering that most childcarers are very low paid and are either self employed or work for voluntary organisations with very limited means.

Resources for Training

The quality of care provided for young children and the status of childcare work generally is unlikely to improve in any significant way without considerable investment in training. It is up to both local authorities and central government to consider how they can best provide the necessary resources to make it possible for childcare workers to have real access to SVQs and to any other worthwhile training opportunities developed locally.

Introducing regulatory and monitoring controls on childcare workers and insisting on a triennial Review of services designed to identify weaknesses in service provision, whilst important aspects of a system for improving the standards of care available to children, can only have a frustratingly limited effect and may even be damaging if they are not accompanied by the resources necessary to take remedial action where inadequacies in the system arise. Training is of fundamental importance in the process of raising the standards of childcare and meeting those inadequacies in the long term.

From the analysis contained in this book of the first Review of Services for Under Eights undertaken in Scotland, the Review has been shown to be a potential catalyst for fundamental change and development of far reaching significance in the way services for early years are planned and delivered.

It is obvious, even from the first Review, that change is beginning to take place – the initial and most basic change lies in a recognition that a coherent co-ordinated policy framework is required to underpin future service developments in early years work. In line with this is a recognition that organisational structures in local authorities require to adapt to facilitate the kind of inter-agency working and collaboration on provision of services the Act requires.

However, the changes brought about by the Review and by the wider requirements of the Children Act itself have to be seen in the larger context of the major changes in family living which have occurred in the last thirty years and the fundamental shift in thinking on how best to respond to the needs of young children living in today's communities, using the UN Convention on the Rights of the Child as the basis for an underpinning philosophy which places the needs of the child at the core of the response. The Children Act is an attempt to take account of these changes and provide a framework for the protection of young children, giving local authorities the responsibilities of carrying through the intentions of the legislation.

However, if it is right that the Act requires local authorities to start from the premise that children's needs come first and to make an appropriate response couched within an inter-agency framework and corporate policies, then it is reasonable to argue, by extension, that such a response is also right for central government. As things presently stand, however, there is no co-ordinated strategy for improving and developing provision at a national level. Central government is still hamstrung by fragmented responsibility for young children spread across several departments, and a predominant philosophy which places responsibility for childcare, other than in cases of obvious and severe need, formally at the door of parents. So long as this situation prevails central government will be unable to mirror nationally what it is requiring of local authorities through the Children Act. The implementation of a comprehensive, publicly funded childcare strategy requires a review of national policy and a consequent injection of adequate resources to provide for Children in Scotland. Until that time the ability of local authorities to make the best use of the Reviews to improve the range and the standard of childcare in their communities is severely limited.

The first Review of Services for Under Eights has provided very powerful arguments for a properly co-ordinated, publicly funded childcare service for young children in Scotland. As noted by Cllr Elizabeth Maginnis in her overview to Chapter 1: "It is clear that an unambiguious commitment to more resources is essential if services to the under eights are to be coherently developed."

BIBLIOGRAPHY

REVIEWS

1. Borders Regional Council Education Department and Social Work Department *Review Of Services For Children Under Eight* (August 1992)

2. Central Regional Council *Services for Children Under Eight - The Children Act 1989, Review of Childminding, Daycare and Education Services for Children Under Eight.* (February 1993)

3. Dumfries and Galloway Regional Council - *Review Of Services for Children Under Eight.*

4. Fife Regional Council - *The Children Act 1989 Section 19 Review Report* (October 1992)

5. Grampian Regional Council - *Review Of Day Care Services For Under Eights* (January 1993)

6. Highland Regional Council's - *Review Of Day Care Provision For Children Under Eight Years Of Age*

7. Lothian Regional Council - *Children Act 1989 Section 19 Review Of Daycare Services Children Under Eight* (February 1993)

8. Strathclyde Regional Council - *Review of Childminding, Daycare and Education Services For Children Under Eight* (February 1993)

9. Tayside Regional Council, Social Work Department and Education Department - *Review of Childminding Daycare and Education Services For Children Under Eight In Tayside* (February 1993)

10. Orkney Islands Council, Social Work Department & Education Department - *A Review of Provision Of Services for Children Under Eight* (1993)

11. Shetland Islands Council Social Work Department & Education Department - *A Review Of Provision For Children Under Eight* (1993)

12. Western Isles Council - *Review Of Day Services For Children Under Eight* (1993)

13. London Borough Of Sutton - *Children Act 1989 Review Of Day Care Draft For Consultation* (September 1992)

14. Birmingham City Council Social Services Department - *Review Of Daycare Services In The City Of Birmingham For Children Aged Under Eight* (1993)

M. Hillman Ed Children, Transport and the Quality of Life PSI (1993)

Andersson, Benjt-Erik (1992)
Effects of daycare on cognitive and socio-emotional competence of thirteen year old Swedish school children, *Child Development* 63, pp 20-36

Blackburne, L. (1992), Nursery Children Get Head Start, Times Educational Supplement, July 24

Jowett, S. and Sylva K. (1986), *Does Kind of Pre-school Matter?*, Educational Research 28, No. 1

Schweinhart, L., Weikert, C. and Larner, M. (1986), *Consequences of three pre-school curriculum models through age 15*, Early Education Research Quarterly, 15-43

Brown, U. and Tait, L. (1992) *Working Miracles*. Glasgow: Scottish Low Pay Unit

Cohen, B. (1990) *Caring for Children: The 1990 Report*. Family Policy Study Centre

General Register Office (1991) *Census Monitor for Tayside Region*. Edinburgh

Hennessy, S., Martin, S., Moss, P. and Melhuish, E. (1992) *Children and Day Care*. London: Chapman

Payline, 14 (1992) *Low Pay in the Scottish Regions in 1992*. Scottish Low Pay Unit, Glasgow

Sylvia, K. (1991) *Educational Aspects of Day Care in Moss and Melhuish (ed.) Current Issues in Day Care for Young Children*. London: HMSO

INDEX

After school care   25, 61, 63, 96

Babysitters   39
Borders Early Years Voluntary Sector
    Forum   83
Borders Health Board   84-84
Borders Region
    data collection   68-69
    evaluation of process   70-71
    implementation of Act   66-67
    lessons learnt from changes 69-70, 71-72
    provisions prior to Act   65-66
    Review process   67-69
    strategies for Review   11-12
Borders SPPA   65, 83-84

Central Region
    strategies for Review   19-20
childminders   2, 25, 61
    see also daycare, Scottish Childminding
    Association
children
    and housing   1
    and independence   2
Children Act 1989   ix, 2
    funding for implementation   x, 9, 12, 14,
                                 33, 39, 42, 67, 71, 72
    in Scotland   ix-x, 2-3, 56
    local authority role   x, 105-106
    research on   4

review requirements   3
    see also Children Act Review, Scottish
    Office
Children Act Review
    benefits of involvement   106
    degree of standardisation   104
    funding   4, 7, 10, 58, 67, 101, 102
    future reviews   xi, 8-9, 15, 34-35,
                                 57-58, 111
    local authority aims   x, 8, 101, 102-103
    local authority difficulties 4, 6, 102, 105
    regional approaches   7-22
    responsibility for   3
    Scottish Office guidelines   3, 6, 8, 40, 58,
                                 67, 105, 109
    summing up   101-117
    time constraints   4, 8, 102
Children in Scotland Early Years
    Development Project   4, 11
Community Care   4, 35, 67, 112
Cothrom Centre South Uist   98
consultation   x, 8, 74, 109-111
    with councils   103. 105-106
    with voluntary and other agencies   74-100,
                                 107-108, 109-110
    with parents and public   110-111
    with health boards   77-78, 84, 85-86, 110
    see also individual regions
creches   25, 61

Daycare   *x, 3, 7, 36, 51, 52, 85-86, 87*
see also after school care, babysitters,
childminders, creches, nannies, nursery
education, pre-school services, Scottish Pre-
School Play Association, under eights

Ethnic minorities   *2, 8, 30, 36, 47, 48,*
61, 62, 96, 112-113

Family Matters   *11, 68, 72, 83, 84*
Fife Play Partnership   *89-92*
Fife Region
  consultations   *89-92*
  strategies for Review   *19*

Gaelic playgroups   *24, 98*
Glasgow City Council
  Parks and Recreation   *78*
Grampian Region
  strategies for implementation of Act   *18-19*
  strategies for Review   *17*
Grampian SPPA   *92-94*
Guidelines *see* Scottish Office

Highland Region
  consultation   *52-55, 57-58*
  implications of Review   *56-57*
  lessons from Review   *57-58*
  report   *55-56*
  Review process   *51-56*
Highland SPPA   *52, 55, 81-83*
Highlands and Islands
  geographical difficulties   *14, 51, 58*
housing
  'child unfriendly'   *1*

Inter agency/departmental collaboration
3, 10, 11, 57, 59, 74, 83, 85-86,
87, 92, 103, 104-105, 107-109

Lanarkshire Health Board   *77-78*

local government reorganisation   *4, 11, 33,*
94, 106
Lothian Community Child Health   *85-86*
Lothian Region
  analysis of Review   *62-63*
  consultation   *62*
  data collection   *60-62*
  lessons from Review   *63-64*
  policy aims and objectives   *60*
  prior joint working arrangements   *59*
  Review process   *60-63*
  views on Review   *20-22*
Lothian SPPA   *87-88*

Nannies   *2, 39*
Nurseries and Childminders Regulation
  Act 1948   *2, 24*
nursery education
  in Europe   *1*
  in Scotland   *1*
  in Strathclyde   *10-11, 24*
  see also pre-school services

One parent families   *1, 36, 58, 97, 114*
  see also women
One Plus Strathclyde   *94-97*
Orkney Islands Council
  involvement in Review   *16-17*

Partners in Learning   *34*
policy development   *106-109, 116-117*
pre-school services
  and working mothers   *2*
  need for   *2, 33-37*
  private sector   *2, 20, 21, 22, 61, 63, 92*
  value of   *ix, 1, 37*
  voluntary sector   *10, 17, 18, 20,*
21, 25, 34, 63, 66
  see also daycare

Quality of care   *33, 37, 56, 79, 81,*
86, 88, 96, 98-99, 114-115

Registration requirements for Scotland   *3, 4*

rural areas   *6, 12, 51, 58, 103, 110, 113*

Scotlands Children: Proposals for Child Care
   Policy and Law   *1, 72*

Scottish Childminding Association

   Highland Region   *80-81*

   Strathclyde   *77*

Scottish Independent Nurseries Association *27*

Scottish Office

   guidance   *3, 6, 8, 40, 58, 67, 105, 109*

   Scottish Pre-School Play Association
      26, 52, 55, 65, 76-77,
      78-80, 81-83, 83-84,
      87-88, 91, 92-94

Shetland Islands

   benefits of Review   *15*

special interest groups   *8, 114*

special needs   *2, 8, 48, 52, 61,*
      62, 75, 86, 112, 115

SPPA *see* Scottish Pre-School Play Association

Stepping Stones in Scotland   *27, 97-98*

'stranger danger'   *1*

Strathclyde Childminding Association   *27*

Strathclyde Early Years Voluntary Sector

Forum   *74-76, 95*

Strathclyde Link Up Development and
   Training   *26*

Strathclyde Playscheme Working Party   *27*

Strathclyde SPPA   *26, 76-77*

Strathclyde Region

   background information   *23-26*

   consultation   *30-31, 32, 33*

   data collection   *29-30*

   future policy and services   *32-34*

   future reviews   *34-35*

   implementing Review   *26-27*

   pre-school services   *24-25, 34*

   Review process   *27-32*

   strategies for Review   *9-11, 25, 27, 28*

Tayside Health Board   *35, 80*

Tayside Region

   background information   *35-38*

   daycare needs   *36-37*

   daycare provision prior to Act   *37-38*

   inter-agency working group   *39-40*

   interdepartmental advisory group   *43-45*

   implementing Act   *43-49*

   Joint Report   *40-42*

   information strategy   *46-47*

   lessons from Review   *49-50*

   outcome of Review   *50-51*

   strategies for Review   *12-14*

   Review process   *43, 45-47, 48, 49*

Tayside SPPA   *78-80*

training   *x, 34, 71, 75, 79, 84, 96, 115*

   resources for   *34, 115-116*

UN Convention on the Rights of the Child
      107, 116

under eights

   Borders Region   *11, 71*

   Central Region   *20*

   Grampian Region   *17, 18-19*

   Highland Region   *16, 55*

   Lothian Region   *20, 22, 59, 60, 63*

   Orkney   *16-17*

   Strathclyde   *9-10, 24, 32-33*

   Tayside   *40-41*

   Western Isles   *15*

   see also daycare

Voluntary and other agencies   *107-108,*
      109-110

   consultation experiences   *74-100*

Western Isles

   involvement in Review process   *14-15*

women

   and paid employment   *2, 36-37*

   and training   *99*

CLYDEBANK · DISTRICT LIBRARY

HMSO publications are available from:

HMSO Bookshops
71 Lothian Road, Edinburgh, EH3 9AZ
031-228 4181 Fax 031-229 2734

49 High Holborn, London, WC1V 6HB
071-873 011 Fax 071-873 8200 (counter service only)

258 Broad Street, Birmingham, B1 2HE
021-643 3740 Fax 021-643 6510

33 Wine Street, Bristol, BS1 2BQ
0272 264306 Fax 0272 294515

9-21 Princess Street, Manchester, M60 8AS
061-834 7201 Fax 061-833 0634

16 Arthur Street, Belfast, BT1 4GD
0232 238451 Fax 0232 235401

HMSO Publications Centre
(Mail, fax and telephone orders only)

PO Box 276, London, SW8 5DT
Telephone orders 071-873 9090

General enquiries 071-873 0011
(queuing system in operation for both numbers)

Fax orders 071-873 8200

HMSO's Accredited Agents
(see Yellow Pages)
and through good booksellers

Printed in Scotland for HMSO by CC No 6033 10C 9/94

ST